COSMIC
HABIT
FORCE

COSMIC HABIT FORCE

How to *Discover* and *Use Nature's Superpower*

MITCH HOROWITZ

author of *The Miracle Club*

MEDIA

Published 2023 by Gildan Media LLC
aka G&D Media
www.GandDmedia.com

First Paperback Edition: 2023

Front cover design by Tom McKeveny

Interior design by Meghan Day Healey of Story Horse, LLC.

Library of Congress Cataloging-in-Publication Data is available upon request

ISBN: 978-1-7225-0633-9

10   9   8   7   6   5   4   3   2   1

CONTENTS

INTRODUCTION

"Behind the Lines"
The Natural Force of Habit

This book is inspired by the teachings of pioneering success author Napoleon Hill (1883–1970). It centers on Hill's late-career teaching of Cosmic Habit Force, which I consider one of his most complete, powerful, and practical ideas. Cosmic Habit Force is the teaching of Hill's by which I am most personally inspired, and I build upon and explore his outlook throughout this book. I believe that this exploration not only provides a unique key to Hill's system, but also functions as a blueprint to living with effectiveness, ability, and maximal self-expression.

Hill's work and inspiration underscore this book. Its ideas are my own as a dedicated and lifelong student.

Seen in a certain sense, Cosmic Habit Force is the "secret" that Hill said he concealed no less than one hundred times in *Think and Grow Rich*. To state the secret flat out, Hill wrote, would deprive the reader of the fruitful effort involved in finding and learning to apply it. At the same time, Hill did not intend to play coy with his readers. With that in mind, I believe we can embark on a transparent and applicable exploration of his secret, which is, in a sense, the secret to fulfillment itself.

I reference this secret not to sound mysterious but to describe a facet of life that is frequently overlooked and even undiscovered yet is also vividly clear. Hill references his secret in the chapter on "Imagination" in *Think and Grow Rich*:

Strange and paradoxical as it may seem, the "secret" is NOT A SECRET. Nature, herself, advertises it in the earth on which we live, the stars, the planets suspended within our view, in the elements above and around us, in every blade of grass, and every form of life within our vision.

Nature advertises this "secret" in the terms of biology, in the conversion of a tiny cell, so small that it may be lost on the point of a pin, into the HUMAN BEING now reading this line. The conversion of desire into its physical equivalent is, certainly, no more miraculous!

I have written about Hill's secret before, and there are different ways of stating it. But all of them refer back to one basic truth: *you experience innate and inevitable power when you enter into natural alignment with laws that enable the growth and maintenance of all life*. This is not dissimilar to concepts found within Taoism and Transcendentalism. Once you function within this cosmic flow, cycles of growth appear in your life. You become like the seedling that eventually bursts through the soil. All of nature aids your progress. This is not because you are somehow elevated or advanced but simply because you are operating within innate cycles of growth and production.

With the cultivation of right habits and choices— which means sustained, generative conduct and activity—you merge with reproductive, cyclical, and natural laws. As will be seen, these laws also possess a metaphysical or extra-material dimension. Barring some equally powerful intervention, these laws deliver you to the destination you intently seek.

This book helps you select among and live within those transcendentally and physically harmonious habits and choices. The 23 "cosmic habits" in this book are not direct echoes of what appears within the work of Napoleon Hill.* You do not need a new book to retread old ground. Rather, these habits are fresh—but also faithful—soundings of themes and imperatives found in Hill's work and that members of my Master Mind group, as well as devotees of Hill's writing from all stations of life, have committedly worked with.** Each habit is presented in a manner that I hope addresses your most urgently felt needs, as well as broader demands that characterize our present era. Taken together, these 23 steps are an applied program in Cosmic Habit Force. They ultimately synchronize you with cycles, inevitabilities, and forces that bring growth to our world and to you as an individual. In that sense, Cosmic Habit Force can feel like a causative energy at the back of your efforts—which, in fact, it is.

The approach that I have described—cultivation of generative habits and actions—is not only a formula for accomplishment, but it is the best lifestyle I personally know of for individual happiness. We are conditioned

---

* Twenty-three is a number of synchronous significance to artists and spiritual thinkers who I admire, although do not always agree with, including Robert Anton Wilson, William S. Burroughs, Genesis P-Orridge, Aleister Crowley, and Arthur Koestler.

** If you are unfamiliar with the concept of a Master Mind group, see Appendix III: Napoleon Hill's 17 Laws of Success.

to think in terms of elusive or inflated concepts when we consider self-development and its horizons. People of a spiritual orientation might employ terms like *realized, enlightened,* or *illumined.* I personally find such language overused and, based on observation, excessive. People of a psychological bent may use terms like *well-adjusted, actualized,* or *fulfilled.* Those concepts are perhaps more graspable; but, like the recent vocabulary of cognitive-behavioral therapy, psychological terminology can proscribe the individual to a life of diagnostic contentment rather than encourage and support a more expansive sense of attainment.

For my part, I contend, and I believe that Hill's work affirms, that *the true aim of life is maximum self-expression.*

Individualized expression occurs often, though not always, through livelihood or personal aim. These are sometimes the same and sometimes different. It is important to note that Hill's program is not strictly about careerism or money-making; it is about the *concretization of ideas.* Yet in his landmark *Think and Grow Rich,* Hill also acknowledged, with an admirable absence of sentimentality, that "money and material things are essential for freedom of body and mind." Anyone who doubts that has probably never known lack. Voluntarily or periodically eschewing money is not the same as suffering its true absence. If you grew up in the shadow of need, as I did, you probably have no doubts about the reality of what I have just stated.

Hill put it this way in a 1952 lecture he delivered as part of his Success Unlimited class: "I have never yet found any way of getting along in life in any station or calling above mediocrity without financing, and I don't believe anybody else can do it."

Hill's philosophy is not lacking ideals—but it confronts life and its material element with complete realism. This is why Hill's sharpest critics in journalism and academia—although not without valid points (and I have criticized Hill myself *)—tend to reveal a subtle sense of social entitlement when categorizing programs of self-striving and money-making as culturally retrograde, superficial, or misleading. Part of why sectors of opinion-shaping media and academia lag in understanding self-help movements and practical spirituality, or evince criticism aforethought of such movements, stems, I believe, from social class and unfamiliarity with need. Wage and commission earners experience needs that many cultural commentators never have or will. And they are wholly canny toward and capable of evaluating the outcome of their efforts toward self-development.

---

* E.g., see my *One Simple Idea: How Positive Thinking Reshaped Modern Life* (2014).

* * *

Like money, self-expression is most keenly yearned for in its absence. A deficit of self-expression can leave even the emotionally and financially secure person with a chronic if undefined sense of regret, ennui, and anxiety. Experience has led me to believe that the absence of ability to express your selfhood—to see through some significant measure of your creative ideals and wishes, as well as the ability to reasonably manage immediate and long-term events toward desired ends—results in a considerable range of what are today regarded as emotional disorders. Our lives and needs are complex and require many sustaining elements, mentally, emotionally, and physically. But in three decades as a seeker, writer, and fitful student of life, I have observed that there exists no greater and more direct route to vitality, self-respect, hopeful expectancy, and conviviality than the expression of and movement toward your most deep-seated personal wishes. Scan the events of your life and determine whether you disagree.

If you share my instinct that self-expression, as I have just described it, is critical to your sense of individuality, and if you agree that material wellbeing is also necessary for healthful selfhood, then it stands to reason that your wish to be a productive being—to be, in spiritual terms, a person reflective of the image of creation or, as the ancient Hermetic dictum puts it, "as above, so below"—requires a methodology or system by which to attain actualized self-conception. That system is Cosmic Habit Force. It is, as alluded, the cycle of repeat behaviors that place you in flow with the growth, maintenance, and renewal of the whole of nature. This means living as part of the organic patterns and sustaining modes that govern all of life. Referencing Cosmic Habit Force in a 1963 lecture, Hill said, "This is the law by which the equilibrium of the whole universe is maintained in orderliness through established habits."

I should note that Hill developed or at least named his theory of Cosmic Habit Force several years after publishing *The Law of Success* in 1928 and *Think and Grow Rich* in 1937. Hill noted that while Cosmic Habit Force is the conceptual underpinning of both books, this particular framing did not occur to him when he wrote them. In 1952, he related this story to a class:

> Some years ago, shortly after *Think and Grow Rich* was published, I began to get letters and telegrams from all over the world complimenting me on that marvelous book. And those letters and telegrams became so numerous that I sent my secretary out and got a copy of it. I hadn't read it since I wrote it

some year and a half before that. And I sat down and read it. I read it carefully. And while I was reading, I discovered in that book, not on the lines but behind the lines, this marvelous subject on which we're speaking tonight, the law of Cosmic Habit Force . . . Cosmic Habit Force is a law of the universe into which all of the other natural laws blend and become a part. It's the comptroller of all of the natural laws, you might say.

Hill's earliest references to Cosmic Habit Force appeared in his books *The Master Key to Riches* in 1945 and *Think Your Way to Wealth* in 1948. In the latter book, Hill wrote:

Cosmic Habit Force is the particular application of energy with which nature maintains the existing relationship between the atoms of matter, the stars and planets, the seasons of the year, night and day, sickness and health, life and death, and more important to us right now, it is the medium through which all habits and all human relationships are maintained, the medium through which thought is translated into its physical equivalent.

You, of course, know that nature maintains a perfect balance between all the elements of matter and energy throughout the universe. You can see the stars and planets move with perfect precision, each keeping its own place in time and space, year-in and year-out. You can see the seasons of the year come and go with perfect regularity. You can see that night and day follow each other in unending regularity.

To this schema, he added: "We are ruled by habits, all of us. Our habits are fastened upon us by repetition of thought and experience, therefore, we can control our earthly destinies just to the extent that we control our thoughts." This is a critical aspect of Hill's analysis.

Although there exists no clinical consensus on exactly how habits are formed, there is general agreement that habits can be altered. And, significantly, the relatively recent field of neuroplasticity uses magnetic resonance imaging (MRI) to reveal that behavioral alteration itself changes neural pathways through which electrical impulses travel in your brain. Hence, personal agency not only alters conduct but the physical organism itself. This adds greater weight to another statement that Hill made in the 1963 lecture quoted earlier, in which he emphasized the individual's role in Cosmic Habit Force: "Man is the only living creature that is equipped with the power of choice by which he may establish his own thought patterns or break up and rearrange them at will." Without the benefit of neuroscience, Hill grasped the self-reinforcing dynamic of habits and of how a habit, once set, proceeds according to a kind of organic automaticity.

In a similar vein, Hill wrote in *The Master Key to Riches*: "The law of Cosmic Habit Force is Nature's method of giving fixation to all habits so that they may carry on automatically once they have been set into motion—the habits of men the same as the habits of the universe. . . . Cosmic Habit Force is the principle by which all habits are fixed and made permanent in varying degrees."*

Everything that I have just observed applies to positive and productive as well as negative and self-defeating habits. This book deals not only with generative habits that maintain and enhance life, but also with the revision of certain habits that deplete and despoil our capacities for attainment and expression, such as chronic fear. Cosmic Habit Force is also a powerful tool in rebounding from failure and setback. Hill called failure a necessary course-correction. Within the scheme of Cosmic Habit Force, failure shatters calcified, unsuccessful thought patterns, approaches, and relationships. It is an engine of growth. It can be painful. But without friction, rejection, and opposition we would never revise misplaced or incomplete efforts or questionable ties and life directions.

---

* For further reference, I have included abridgments of Hill's chapters on Cosmic Habit Force from *The Master Key to Riches* and *Think Your Way to Wealth* in, respectively, appendices I and II.

For the reasons that we have been considering, Hill in *The Master Key to Riches* called Cosmic Habit Force "the comptrolling principle of the entire philosophy." I want this book to serve as a manual in using the teacher's all-encompassing method. I believe that what you find here supplies the key—and, with it, a sense of personal advantage—to using Hill's inner system. My aim is to provide the steps that harness Hill's most esoteric insights into a methodology that delivers you to your highest self-conception.

Nature is inclined toward growth—and also toward decay, which itself is part of the process of renewal. Without death and renewal, resources would deplete. Life would be unsustainable. Like nature, you, me, and everyone reading these words will experience decline and eventual demise. My deepest wish is that by enacting the habits in this book, and entering the cycles into which they integrate you, you will, barring some equally powerful countervailing event or force, prove capable of approaching finality with the satisfaction of having lived out some measure of your essential purpose.

I must finally note that I write this book, as with all my books, solely as a seeker. And, in this case, as a student of Hill's work. I am not a clinician, guru, life coach, therapist, or teacher. I am on the path with you, experimenting with and experiencing Hill's ideas. We are co-students. I seek no other designation than someone who writes with the wish that you and I together reach our higher possibilities through the application of practical philosophy.

HABIT 1

PMA for Real

The cultivation of a Positive Mental Attitude, or PMA, is the starting point of Cosmic Habit Force. In a 1952 talk on Cosmic Habit Force, Napoleon Hill said: "As I have called to your attention so many times, nature has given to every individual the most precious thing available to mankind, and this thing which has been given to mankind by nature has never been given to any other living creature. And it is nothing more nor less than the power of control over one's own mind."

Depending on your temperament, PMA can come naturally or fitfully. For me, it is the latter. I am not by nature optimistic. I am anxious by temperament, something probably reinforced by conditioning and family background, as most personality traits are. Anxiety can be burdensome and distracting. That is among my personal reasons for dedicating myself to the study and practice of positive-mind metaphysics. For me, it is a lifelong effort.

I am aware that something as benign sounding as a Positive Mental Attitude can seem like weak tea in a world teeming with stresses, aggravators, social injustice, and myriad complexities. But look again. Although some of Hill's earliest references to PMA appeared in *The Master Key to Riches* in 1945, I was turned onto the concept from a very different source: the pioneering D.C.-based punk band Bad Brains. One of the group's guiding lights, lead singer and song writer H.R. (for Human Rights), discovered Napoleon Hill during his adolescence in Washington, D.C., in the 1970s. It changed everything for the fiercely independent youth and future musical innovator.

In 2017, H.R. told writer Michael Friedman, Ph.D., in *Psychology Today*:

> I was doing more drugs and living wild. At that time, I knew in my heart that I wanted a better way. Just in the nick of time, God taught me how to relate to him. It was in 1979. My father introduced me to a book called *Think and Grow Rich*. So, I read the book

and found the connection to God . . . it introduced a new philosophy to me. The new philosophy was PMA. Anything the mind can conceive and believe, the mind can achieve.

More recently a resident of Baltimore, H.R. in 2015 told John Barry of the *Baltimore City Paper* what PMA and *Think and Grow Rich* meant to him: "It was saying, if you do it in your mind, if you get your mind right, you can do anything. It had this dramatic change in my life. I decided I would use it in my day-to-day living and I would put the lyrics and the message in the songs."

The artist kept his word. He formed a fusion band in 1976 called Mind Power—but soon took matters in a more hardcore direction when the group changed its name to Bad Brains. The inspiration, he explained, came from the Ramones' song "Bad Brain" and the perception that *bad* is street code for *good*. In early 1982, the quartet Bad Brains released its eponymously titled debut album on cassette—a recording that is now considered one of the landmarks of punk and hardcore. Layered with reggae and jazz influences, it is ultimately unclassifiable. The album's keynote is the guitar-thrashing "Attitude" with the lyrics:

> *Don't care what they may say*
> *We got that attitude!*

Don't care what you may do
We got that attitude!

Hey, we got that PMA!
Hey, we got the PMA!

In tribute, I have a lightning bolt with the letters PMA—the band's insignia—tattooed on my left bicep.

H.R. provided a case study of PMA in a 2019 oral history of his life, *Finding Joseph I*:

The theory that Napoleon Hill had in that book, *Think and Grow Rich*, made me rethink the negative things in my life and put them out of my mind, put my strength into being positive, and that's what I did. I worked the theory and put it into practice to see if it would really happen, and it happened. My life changed. Also, a lot of times the youth would come to me and tell me they understood what I was going through and to hold on. They gave me the will to survive and supported me and have a lot to do with this, me getting through the hard times. The youth understood.

Hence, when critics sometimes suggest that Napoleon Hill's fans can be placed into one easy category or box of materialist self-seeking, I tell them: you have no idea.

This gives a sense of Hill's range of influence. Now, let me return to the centrality of PMA to Hill's outlook. Hill continued in his 1952 talk:

Everything that has life in this world, with the lone exception of man, comes into life with its lifespan and its actions and reactions fixed in a definite pattern, through what we call instinct. Man is the only one who comes to life with no fixed pattern, and with the ability to establish and carry out his own pattern, by adapting himself to this great law of Cosmic Habit Force. And in the thought habits of individuals, which are automatically fixed and made permanent by Cosmic Habit Force, no matter whether they are negative or positive. The individual creates the pattern of his thoughts by repetition of thought on any give subject. But the law of Cosmic Habit Force takes over these patterns and makes them permanent unless they are broken up by the will of the individual. Man is the only living creature that is equipped with the power to rearrange these at will.

There are, of course, periods when PMA feels very distant. And, indeed, it is sometimes irresistible or even imperative to voice objections, needs, and protests. This, too, is part of life and it has a legitimate claim on us. But our experiment in this program is to determine *the fullest extent to which our needs can be framed in ways that are affirming of possibility and utility rather than as repetitive complaints* in which we are so heavily conditioned to indulge. I grew up in an atmosphere where complaining formed the basis of most conversation. I realized only later how routinized, self-defining, and encompassing complaining can become. Although fruitless, complaining can feel very normal. PMA healthfully disrupts that.

Positivity sometimes means repose rather than action. There may be moments when forward-moving paths simply do not present themselves. In such cases, rather than making one more entreaty to someone or attempting one more futile angle on a problem, we may need to wait and improve our skills, knowing that cyclical changes in social, intimate, or commercial settings are as inevitable as those observed in nature. In that sense, I want to propose an exercise that you may have seen before in hopes that this chapter will move you to reenter it. Or, if you are encountering it for the first time, I hope that you will find it deeply revelatory. It is called the 30-Day Mental Challenge.

This exercise is based on a passage from a 1931 book, *Body, Mind, and Spirit* by Elwood Worcester and Samuel McComb. The two Episcopal ministers ran an innovative, religiously based healing program in Boston in the early twentieth century. In their book, a prominent scientist described radically improving his life through a one-month thought experiment. I have condensed his testimony:

> Up to my fiftieth year I was unhappy, ineffective, and obscure. I had read some New Thought literature and some statements of William James on directing one's attention to what is good and useful and ignoring the rest.* Such ideas seemed like bunk— but feeling that life was intolerable I determined to subject them to a month-long test.
>
> During this time, I resolved to impose definite restrictions on my thoughts. In thinking of the past, I would dwell only on its pleasing incidents. In thinking of the present, I would direct attention to its desirable elements. In thinking of the future, I would regard every worthy and possible ambition as within reach.
>
> I threw myself into this experiment. I was soon surprised to feel happy and contented. But the outward changes astonished me more. I deeply craved the recognition of certain eminent men. The foremost of these wrote me, out of the blue, inviting me to become his assistant. All my books were published. My colleagues grew helpful and cooperative.

---

* New Thought is an umbrella term for the positive-mind tradition, which I use several times in this book.

It seems that I stumbled upon a *path of life* and set forces working for me which were previously working against me.

I stumbled upon a path of life. Sit with that line. It is the keynote of PMA.

Let us repeat this experiment together: 1) Choose your start date (you can make it today, at this moment); 2) write out the speaker's full quoted testimony by hand (never underestimate the value of that); and 3) add: "I dedicate myself on this day of _____ to focus on all that is nourishing, advancing, and promising for thirty days (signed) _____"

That's it. If you fall off course during the 30 days—and that is inevitable—do not be concerned. Do not feel the need to start over. Simply return to your passage and oath and resume your activities. I can promise you: I have received remarkable testimonies from people about the power of this exercise. I personally began a new round the day that I wrote these words. It is an exercise that bears continually reapproaching. Something new will almost always be gleaned.

As alluded, PMA does not imply some perfumed or artificial attitude toward life. It is very different from forced optimism. The extraordinary spiritual philosopher P.D. Ouspensky (1878–1947) made the following observation to his students in his posthumously published 1986 book *A Further Record: Extracts from Meetings 1928–1945.* In common parlance, the philosopher said,

> . . . a positive attitude does not really mean a positive attitude, it simply means liking certain things. A really positive attitude is something quite different. Positive attitude can be defined better than positive emotion, because it refers to thinking. But a real positive attitude includes in itself understanding of the thing itself and understanding of the quality of the thing from the point of view, let us say, of evolution and those things that are obstacles. Things that are against, i.e., if they don't help, they are not considered, they simply don't exist, however big they may be externally. And by not seeing them, i.e., if they disappear, one can get rid of their influence. Only, again it is necessary to understand that not seeing wrong things does not mean indifference; it is something quite different from indifference.

What the teacher is saying, albeit on a vast scale, is that the individual must seek to understand forces that develop or erode his humanity. This effort places the seeker in front of an immense question. Hence, we are not principally concerned here with conventions of good or bad, or happy or sad, but with questions of *developmental forces*, the theme to which this book is, in its way, dedicated.

From time to time, I hear from old friends, and sometimes strangers, wondering why I occupy myself with what they regard as "woo-woo" stuff—that is, New Thought and positive-mind traditions.

They are right about my commitments. Since the 2014 publication of my *One Simple Idea*, a history and analysis of positive-mind metaphysics, I have grown more dedicated to exploring the use and viability of PMA or the mind-power thesis, which is: *thoughts are causative.*

My aim is not to disembark from "serious" esoteric traditions (more on which in a moment); nor is it to discontinue my work as a historian of alternative spirituality. Rather, I am specifically interested in formulating a tough-minded, intellectually defensible, and useful distillation of positive-mind principles. I try to locate the ancient antecedents for mind power in Hermeticism and a wide range of religious traditions, as well as in modern expressions such as Transcendentalism, Idealism, Pragmatism, Christian Science, and the work of nineteenth century experimenters like Phineas Quimby, Emma Curtis Hopkins, and Horatio Dresser, up through twentieth century mystical voices such as Neville Goddard, Vernon Howard, and Ernest Holmes.

But make no mistake: I am not interested in intellectualizing New Thought ideas. I am interested in *using them*. And, if I am able, in helping my co-seekers do the same.

The fact is, I have a deep and abiding love for what are sometimes considered sensationalized works of metaphysics, such as *Think and Grow Rich*, *How to Win Friends and Influence People*, *It Works*, *The Game of Life*, and *Psycho-Cybernetics*, among others. I feel an absolute conviction that many of these popular works possess a touch of the extraordinary. That is, amid certain dead ends, over-reaches, and drama, they also evince tremendous insight, workable ideas, and *a spirituality of results* tested in the experience of the reader.

I cannot always say that about many contemporary expressions of traditional or esoteric spirituality. "There's no short cut," a good man once told me within a learned esoteric community. My response is: "I don't know that." I have not fully tested that thesis. When an individual is starved for understanding—or for the solution to a life-depleting problem—remarkable things become possible. Accelerants may become available. Philosopher William James (1842–1910) wrote about the power of a "conversion experience," which the philosopher described as a realization of a greater truth that objectively reorganizes the facts of outer life. Others speak of "awakening," a term that I find too portentous. Awakening implies permanency, whereas the search for change is often filled with switchbacks and frustration. Of this much I feel certain: the inner key to almost any program of legitimate self-development lies in the *depth of an individual's hunger for self-change*. As an Arab proverb put it: "The way bread tastes depends on how hungry you are."

I have likewise witnessed individuals who have dedicated decades of their lives in the service of serious traditions—yet in a moment of anxiety or even a minor mishap they evince the same brokenness that I do. I ask why. And I ask you the reader (and myself) not to jump to any handy answer. Just hold the question.

I just used the metaphor of "bread." The implication is that a tradition must be nourishing—it must offer lasting sustenance and not anodyne truisms. Can this also be said of New Thought and its adjunct traditions? If so, should you run off and read a popular work like *The Power of Positive Thinking*? Well, my answer is yes.

Positive-thinking traditions are, very simply, *applied Transcendentalism*. The mind-power equation is an effort to live within the stream of creative potency using the medium of thought; to fulfill the dictum of Romans 12:2 by being "transformed by the renewing of your mind;" to use the aspirations of thought as a means of bridging worldly and unseen life; to tap the creative potential inherent in our relation to extra-physical sources, a topic to which I return. Positive-mind metaphysics—and much of the American metaphysical tradition—posits a thin line of separation between mental and spiritual experience. This is the influence of New Thought.

I am committed to New Thought for reasons of spiritual belief. I share Alcoholics Anonymous founder Bill Wilson's ideal that a "Higher Power"—or what I term a "Greater Force"—can bridge gaps, crises, and inabilities in our lives, especially when cognitive efforts fail. This led a critic in the *Wall Street Journal* to contend that "Mr. Horowitz isn't interested in research." I am interested—I explore biological, neurological, and quantum physics research in *The Miracle Club* and elsewhere. But I also believe that a blind spot exists in many of our research models, which is that when we discover a biological or physical correlation to an event, we assume that it must be the only thing going on. We fail to consider that there may be lots of causes and correlates—that the thing occurring biochemically may be triggered by varying factors: physical, psychological, and extra-physical. For one thing, I cite data (sometimes hastily dismissed or overlooked) from decades of academic psychical research.* I may be wrong about

---

* A comprehensive meta-analysis of psychical research data appeared in the flagship journal of the American Psychological Association: "The Experimental Evidence for Parapsychological Phenomena: A Review" by Etzel Cardeña, *American Psychologist*, 2018, Vol. 73, No. 5, 663–677.

extra-physicality; but we do not advance the cause of our understanding by narrowly proscribing the antecedents we consider.

Some seekers have written to me recounting deeply negative experiences at New Thought churches—pointing out a "victim blaming" mentality in which those who suffer illness, accident, tragedy, or setback are subtly held responsible for the "thought patterns" that manifest their woes. These protesters are right. Such attitudes are sometimes voiced. And when they are, I reject them unequivocally. In my *One Simple Idea*, I considered an episode in which *The Secret*'s Rhonda Byrne told an Associated Press reporter that people died in the Holocaust and 9/11 "because their dominant thoughts were on the same frequency of such events." I do not participate in rote criticism of *The Secret*, which I believe has helped millions of people consider the greater possibilities of their minds. But I also believe that Byrne's assessment in this case is flatly wrong. I wrote:

> When facing ultimate moral questions, Byrne ... spoke of the experience of others, describing events that she had never personally encountered or reckoned with. Opinions, like philosophies, demand verification, either by logic or lived experience. Byrne's logic was akin to that of a person visiting a neighbor's house, whistling for a dog, receiving no

response, and concluding that the neighbor has no dog. She took no account of possibilities outside of her purview.

And further:

Spiritual insight arrives through *self-observation*—not in analyzing, or justifying, the suffering experienced *by others*. To judge others is to work without any self-verification, which is the one pragmatic tool of the spiritual search. The private person who can maturely and persuasively claim self-responsibility for *his own* suffering, or who can endure it as an inner obligation, shines a light for others. The person who justifies *someone else's* suffering, in this case through collective fault, only casts a stone.

At the same time, there are gleaming, extraordinary examples—in my life and the lives of co-seekers—of sublime insights, breakthroughs, and concrete results using the mind-power model. This often means harnessing emotive thoughts, visualizations, affirmations, autosuggestion, and prayer to navigate oneself toward a hallowed and deeply thought-through aim. Materialists may call this delusion; but most have not tried it. And most never will. Because spiritual experience is, if it is anything at all, an exquisitely voluntary effort which cannot be learned, opined, received, or otherwise had, or even recognized, in the absence of experience. In a malady of human nature, conviction generally trumps experience.

I personally know journalists and academics who have visited, surveyed, observed and, ultimately, excoriated spiritual communities and traditions without once, even as a personal experiment, engaging in a discrete, hands-on experience, such as meditation. In their minds, to try is to concede intellectual weakness. But the opposite is true.

William James contended that the ultimate test of any ethical or spiritual philosophy is *its effect on conduct.* I have witnessed New Thought methods result in improved conduct and in better, happier, more effective lives. Not flawless lives or lives free of lapses, contradictions, foolishness, or even moments of cruelty and delusion. But nonetheless, a certain dignity and nobility emerges in the life of *one who tries.* And this has driven me to seek out, experiment with, and attempt to communicate the highest truths in New Thought, a modern spiritual tradition that I believe meets the individual directly where he or she lives and that addresses the problems of day-to-day life with utility, grace, and practicality.

In the end, I document and work with positive-mind philosophy, or PMA, because, for all the foibles and weaknesses dotting its history, *it works*. Why does it work? When does it fail? Which methods work? Which do not? What are its blind spots? Why has New Thought done a better job of popularizing versus refining itself? What are its most sublime insights? These questions passionately move me and reappear in these pages.

In the end, my personal approach to studying New Thought, or any spiritual tradition, is captured by martial artist Bruce Lee (1940–1973), who wrote: "Research your own experience; absorb what is useful, reject what is useless and add what is essentially your own."

This informs my study and my search. And I invite you to fashion your own response to it. Hence, PMA is not a template or even a final destination. It is an ethic of self-striving, daily seeking, and mental-emotive fibrousness. It underscores all of our work here.

HABIT 2

A Definite Purpose

"The first place where you want to start using the law of Cosmic Habit Force," Napoleon Hill said in 1952, "is in connection with definiteness of purpose." There may be no more important line in this book.

Reaching a *clarified ideal* of what you want in life, and what your life is dedicated to—Hill called it a Definite Chief Aim, a term he capitalized—is a vital step in honing the fullest qualities of your psyche and efforts. For this to occur, focus and specificity are essential. This mirrors a natural law: focus generates force. Depending on their density, currents of air or water can be waved away or navigated; but if channeled into a condensed stream, the same forces grow irresistible. Light photons are indetectable to the eye; but if condensed into a laser they can sear through hardened matter. There is no reason to assume that self-agency and personal exertion form any exception. We are in a natural state when focused. When we are diffuse in focus, we are diffuse in psyche and effort. In 1888, Friedrich Nietzsche wrote in *The Antichrist*: "Formula for our happiness: a Yes, a No, a straight line, a goal." This is from Walter Kaufmann's translation.

In the same talk that I reference above, Hill provided the following instructions for clarifying your Definite Chief Aim:

1. Write out a complete, clear, and definite statement of your major purpose in life, sign it, and commit it to memory. Then repeat it orally at least once every day and more often if practicable.

2. Write out a clear definite plan by which you intend to begin the attainment of the object of your definite major purpose. State the maximum time allowed for the attainment of that purpose and precisely what service you are willing to give in return for the realization of your purpose.

3. Make your plan flexible enough to permit changes at any time you are inspired to do so.

4. Keep your major purpose and your plans for attaining it strictly to yourself except in connection with your mastermind association.

Personally speaking, my Definite Chief Aim does not have a time element attached to it since it reflects a lifelong aim—everything that I do and labor towards is in its service. Although I encourage you to follow Hill's ideas to the fullest, I realize, as I think he would have, that certain ideas require adapting to personal needs and circumstances. In that vein, people often ask whether it is entirely necessary to attach a dollar amount to an aim, as Hill further prescribed. I have, at various times in my life, applied a dollar amount to my aim and at other times I have opted against listing an amount. My basic aim remains unchanged. And I will, from time to time, rephrase or rewrite my aim to punctuate a certain point, improve clarity, and hone it down.

I believe in informed flexibility. Hence, I sometimes follow Hill's formula to the letter and, for example, determine exactly what I wish to earn, and by when, in connection with my aim; other times I omit a sum. We further explore the question of listing a sum in Habit 21: *When You Meet a Cobra on the Road*.

Life is complex and our needs and expressions are not static. Hence, a seeker must bring his or her own judgment to bear on precisions of application. Never engage in avoidance; definiteness is vital. But I encourage a sense of individual discretion when approaching any teaching.

I am often asked whether an aim must be singular. Doesn't life make multiple demands on us? In the summer of 2021, I received a well-timed note on this question from a thoughtful writer Ross Simonini of Altadena, California. Ross wrote:

> I've heard you speak of well-roundedness as over-rated, but I find that hard to reconcile. Don't you strive to be a good father, partner, writer, teacher, conversationalist, biker, music lover, and editor? Aren't many of these, to some degree, separate aims with separate skills? Or, for you, do they all serve the same aim? (Making money is useful as a partner, but is it really the primary aim?) But also, don't all these different interests inform each other in unexpected ways (such as your Monkees anecdote in *The Miracle Club*) and isn't that diversity useful? Take your interest in the occult: this field of study has the impression of being unified because of the single name, but it's actually a collection of very dispa-

rate subjects from very different people, places and times, studied under a generously sized umbrella: Ufology, meditation, magic, crop circles, spirits, new age, etc . . . In fact, this is what I appreciate about your work—the way you draw connections across divergent ideas, the way you synthesize and syncretize. It reminds me of many thinkers I admire, who are polymaths—and successful ones—who use these varied interests to create whole systems in their work—Steiner, Goethe, Da Vinci, Pythagoras, Avicenna, Newton, Franklin, Wittgenstein, Cocteau, Kant, Lynch, and Hildegaard von Bingen. So: is the single aim all about conceptualizing work in a unified way, even if other people might perceive those aims as different? Twenty-five birds with a single stone? If so, how does one do that?

Ross and I conducted a fruitful back and forth on this question, which he framed with sensitivity. After a time, he wrote me: "Just wanted to let you know that I found your answer in the first few minutes of this show"—it was an episode of the metaphysical talk show Inspire Nation from early 2020. He wrote that he found it "a very satisfying resolution to our correspondence on single aims." Ross's reaction moved me to offer, with a few edits for clarity, the observations that he found resolving:

Having a Definite Chief Aim is my absolute mantra, and I always tell people that if you take one idea from my work, if you take one idea from the work of Napoleon Hill, which has been a great inspiration to me, make it this one: you must have one absolute, focused aim in life. Because focus produces power. Focus and concentration result in power. We see this all the time in nature. You can push air currents out of the way with your hand, as you do all day; but if the vapor of air is focused into a narrow space it becomes as powerful as a bullet. That is literally true and that is a universal truth. So, having a focus brings you psychological, psychical, and intellectual power in ways that cannot be fully summarized. It is necessary to have an absolute, passionate focus in life to which everything else is subservient.

And that is a tough bargain that life strikes with us. Because, as I often say, we all must perform multiple functions in life. We are workers or artists or caregivers; we are sons, daughters, and parents; we are neighbors and spouses. Life requires many roles of us and that is never going to change. But if you scrutinize the lives of your heroes, whoever they may be, you will find that what you treasure and value in those individuals is *the one thing for which they lived*. For Helen Keller, it was human potential; for Nelson Mandela, it was democracy and justice;

for Steve Jobs, it was creating a revolution in hand-held technology, and so on. This is true again and again: if you have one focus, you will heighten your energies in ways that you cannot possibly recognize beforehand. If you take nothing else from any of this work, take that: having one Definite Chief Aim.

The martial artist Bruce Lee, who is a hero to me, said something that I consider an extraordinary insight into human nature and performance: "I fear not the man who has practiced 10,000 kicks once, but I fear the man who has practiced one kick 10,000 times." Take wisdom from that; live with that; sit with that for a period of six months. Having that absolute focus is what makes you exceptional, and it will spill into different areas of your life.

I always tell people who are worried that a focus will make them unbalanced, or that a focus will lead to their neglecting other obligations in life: *one well-chosen focus can cover a lot of different bases.* It may not mean that you get to where you need to go in all of the predictable ways, and in all of the mind's eye ways, and in all of the conventional ways; but one well-chosen focus—whether it's a sport or whether it's artistic or whether it's financial or whether it's martial—will ripple through other facets of life.

One of the great difficulties people face in selecting an aim is their unwillingness to be honest with themselves. We repeat things to ourselves for our whole lives by rote; we think we're being honest but very often these things are reflections of internalized peer pressure, of how we want to appear to ourselves, and of what we think sounds virtuous. We are plagued by these limitations, even within the very private confines of our own thoughts. It is necessary, I believe, to throw away all rote thought, all habitual thought, and ask yourself what you *really want.*

I have a friend who is a lawyer in Washington, D.C., and he attended an Ivy League law school and served a legal fellowship at Princeton. When it was all over, he expected to take a well-paying corporate law job. But he discovered that the hours entailed were just too much. He is interested in international trade, so he took a job instead with the International Trade Commission in D.C., which settles treaty disputes. And he said to me at one point later in life, "You know, I came to realize that my leisure time is really important to me." He's an aficionado of science fiction and role-playing games and Renaissance Fairs and things like that, and whether that's everybody's taste or not it's *his* taste. And he also knew that he had to make a good living; he had to meet his family obligations. But he didn't want to be on a corporate-law fast track, which would dominate every waking aspect of his time. And I really applaud this person because he came down to saying *my leisure time really matters to me; my leisure time is really important to me*. Now, that is not a Definite Chief Aim in itself but it is the kind of honesty that leads you to a definite shape.

Life does not respect halfway measures. Just this morning I was conversing with somebody who is the lead singer of an extraordinary rock band called Starbenders. Her name is Kimi Shelter and we were talking about something I wrote in *Secrets of Self-Mastery*, which is that Revelation 3:16 notes, "So then because thou art lukewarm, and neither cold nor hot, I will spit thee out of my mouth." I think one of the meanings of that statement is that you can be for something or you can be against something, you can run hot or you can run cold, but when you are *lukewarm* you are just taking up space, so to speak; you are not getting anywhere; you are not forwarding or furthering anything; you are drifting. And Kimi pointed out to me that the first song on Starbenders' new album, *Love Potions*, is exactly three minutes and sixteen seconds. And she's had other confluences with the number 316. So, naturally I suggested it as a tattoo. That statement from Revelation inveighing against the lukewarm is something that people should really live with. The lukewarm never get delivered; they never bring us anywhere. That is what I mean when I say that life respects no halfway measures.

It is so rare that we expend anywhere near the limits of our strength. Perhaps we *never* expend the limits of our strength. Hence, we spend our lives underestimating ourselves. If you dedicate yourself to whatever the task is at hand, you discover that you are, in fact, intellectually and often physically capable of overcoming things that you're frightened of. A lot of people experience procrastination. Procrastination is, I believe, fear. But if you throw yourself into the task, not in your mind but actually, you will discover that you are much stronger than you think, particularly when a task is backed by sincere desire. Desire is the engine that drives a Definite Chief Aim. Desire is emotional passion and it is necessary because it will get you past periods where you experience dejection or setback or failure or temporary failure.

My desire to succeed as a historian and writer of alternative spirituality is so strong that it never leaves me. I experience physical exhaustion before I experience a depletion of that desire. Allow that to help you; allow your emotions to help you.

And that means, again, that we must be honest. How many people say, "I want a million dollars"—

but when you drill down, it's not the million dollars that they want; it's freedom, it's the ability to travel, it's more time with their family; it's something that may actually contradict their million-dollar desire. So, if you are not honest, you are stopped cold. In fact, one of the reasons that we do not arrive at a really actionable aim is that we harbor different and sometimes conflicting aims, like wanting a million dollars and working towards a million dollars, but in actuality really wanting travel or leisure time or things that we think the million dollars will facilitate. It is critical not to confuse means with ends. Identify the ends. Following from the ends, we then have the intellectual capacity to ask, "How do I need to get there?" But if you confuse means with ends, everything gets muddled.

It was a great breakthrough for me personally when I was able to be honest with myself about the emotional thrill I experience when I am doing media and speaking publicly. I must be frank, this is no time for B.S. When I get recognized on the street, when somebody asks me to sign a book, well, place whatever label you want on it, it doesn't matter to me, those are emotional peak experiences for me. And being frank with myself about that really came to mean a lot to me. It helped me be much more relaxed. It is important for me to make that admission because our culture takes these admissions away from us. As soon as you make an honest admission, somebody comes along wagging their finger and talking to you about attachment or identification. These are just words. These are just words of which we have a rough consensus-based description. They do not get to the heart of what really motivates a creative, thinking individual, which may be very different for you than for me. But we won't get anywhere with ourselves or with other people until we throw out the catechism, throw out the spiritual vocabulary, stop using that as a kind of call-and-response form of describing life, and actually look at life starting with ourselves and asking, "What do I really want?" It may surprise you.

If we do not earnestly ask this, we dwell in places where we can no longer be served. We spend time in relationships, in workplaces, in friendships, and in family situations that do not serve us, that may even be agonizing for us. I did this for many years. I stuck around work or social situations where I thought. "If only I could make someone see something from my point of view, they would give me the thing I'm looking for." Unfortunately, that almost never occurs. And we lock ourselves into these patterned relationships. It is so helpful to realize that you can walk away from virtually any relationship. There may be consequences; there may be consequences emotionally or financially. I am not denying any of that. But I am saying that it could be profoundly liberating to at least reach the realization that you *can* walk away.

Hence, you must decide what it is you want and you must be brave and sensible about it. Your aim gives you the freedom to prioritize.

I will conclude on something that I quoted earlier from Napoleon Hill: "Make your plan flexible enough to permit changes at any time you are inspired to do so." We will return to this principle in Habit 4: *Flexible Persistence*. But before exploring that, I want to go one step further in considering the power of need and desire.

HABIT 3

The Force of Necessity

How badly do you want what you want? The greatest single factor that delivers you to your goal is a sense of urgency. My friend and co-seeker Lucas Whelan offered this formula for self-change and achievement: "You've got to be in a place that's more painful than growing is." Maybe you have had the experience. A day sometimes arrives when addiction, self-sabotage, self-doubt, or mistreatment at the hands of others finally fills you with such a sense of despair or yearning that the impetus for change naturally arises. It could be one of the most painful but also rewarding days of your life.

We may also face a circumstantial need that hits us with the force of necessity, such as experiencing the wish for financial independence. This struck me when I was fifteen years old. It occurred to me with the impact of absolute truth—what James called a "conversion experience"—that my parents would be unable to support me into young adulthood. I began charting a life plan that would enable some degree of self-sufficiency. I was not after riches, but a meaningful, expansive, and financially sound existence.

Other times, of course, money itself *is* the primary object. Motivational speaker and businessman Jim Rohn wrote in a 1985 book,

> Hey, what if you *had* to be rich? What if the life of someone you love *depended* on your being able to afford the very best medical care?
>
> Let's further suppose that you just learned of a book or a cassette tape that would show you how to make a fortune. Would you buy it? Of course you would!
>
> . . . there are *many* good books and tapes on the subject of creating wealth. But if you don't have to be rich, you probably won't read them or take the time to listen to them. There is an old saying "Necessity is the mother of invention!" How true! With that

in mind always work on your reasons first and the answers second.

Always work on your reasons first and the answers second. The reasons can be—and in order to be real must be—all your own. They require no perfuming or dressing up, an act that separates you from authentic ethics, self-understanding, and driving passion.

As I prepared to work on this section, a member of my Master Mind group emailed me a March 31, 2021, article from *Inc.* magazine entitled, "Science Reveals a Brutal Truth About Pursuing (Much Less Achieving) Certain Goals That Most People Realize Too Late." The author explored several recent social science studies on the efficacy of goal setting. The studies concluded that imbuing your goal with meaning makes its pursuit richer, happier, and more sustainable. The author framed the overall data this way:

> Say you want to earn more money so you can buy a fancier car; the research shows pursuing a material possession-related goal will make you less happy. But if you want to earn more money because you want to save money for your kids to go to college, or help your elderly parents, or to give back to your community . . . now you've given that same goal intrinsic meaning.

As unobjectionable as that sounds, I want to take a careful pause. I have questions about the kinds of studies covered in this article, and specifically about the implication that your aim ought to be reprocessed through some other, presumably higher, purpose. In my experience, the critical thing is that *your goal be starkly self-honest*. Your goal need not be conditioned or attenuated by another person's or group's decisions or proclaimed values. Or by what you think makes you "look good," even if just in your mind's eye, which is often the lens of internalized peer pressure.

In my observation, the factors most likely to deliver you are passion and self-honesty. Apropos of the *Inc.* passage, I have never personally encountered anyone who wants to "earn more money" chiefly to "give back to [his] community." Have you? Now that may be a valid part of someone's goal; but to feel compelled, either internally or publicly, to frame your wishes in shades of altruism can also be an act of sanitizing. Such an act divides you from your authentic necessities and the urgency that accompanies them. What you really want and why are intimate matters. They are for you alone to define. They require no defense or reprocessing.

What's more, I find that many of these contemporary studies of goal setting, human happiness, meaning, and so forth, can be far less complete than headlines make them appear. In reviewing the studies that the journalist cited,

I found that the first one included within it two study groups, the much larger and more significant of which included 64 participants (29 in the active group and 35 in the control group) and involved just three, one-hour group sessions of goal setting conducted across three non-consecutive weeks. I question what such a modest, short-term study can reveal. Even the improved happiness metrics noted in connection with that study—8 and 12 percent within the active group—are so slender that such outcomes would probably be discounted in a pharmaceutical trial. The researchers, however, called these "significant increases." And even accepting the results, who conducted these goal-setting sessions? Is that person skilled at prompting, coaching, encouraging, framing? I sometimes believe that these types of studies measure the efficacy of the clinician more than anything else.

Still, you may wonder what is really at the back of my objections. They are based on a philosophical issue I have with someone else, whether using the mantle of clinical data or moral truisms, *setting values on what you want*. It is human nature to look at what another person wants and categorize it without necessarily understanding what drives that individual, who the person is, where he or she comes from, and what unseen needs a personal aim may fill.

Let's return to Jim Rohn's idea. Rohn is not saying that your sense of necessity cannot be in the service of another. In fact, he specifically names such an example. But he is not framing that example as a ground rule. The critical factor is that your sense of necessity be self-driven and entirely real. Or it will likely fail. That is why necessity matters: *it taps your emotions while also impelling you to consider all avenues of attainment*. That has been my experience, at least. I consider necessity the single greatest factor, though not the only one, in delivering you to your destination.

In the vein of what we just explored, perhaps you have at one time or another been made to feel that your aim is superficial or unrealistic. Well, as alluded, often what an observer perceives as superficial may honor something in you that is unseen, difficult to enunciate, or too intimate to utter. That makes it no less valid. Insofar as realism is concerned, that can be a fair criticism; take it seriously. A real aim is not fantasy. My ground rule is that your aim is real provided you can take *actual steps*, however nascent, toward its fulfillment. The act of progressing toward something, even if incrementally, usually indicates authenticity. If one step brings forth another, realism is probably present.

As suggested in the previous chapter, one healthful and freeing step toward enacting realism and necessity is identifying what is *unnecessary*—and letting it go. The song of necessity is the simplest and most overlooked method of power in your possession. Get rid of everything that runs counter to it.

It is nearly unbelievable how much superfluous activity we engage in. This is often to alleviate boredom, attract attention, or tell other people what to do (a widespread human foible). This problem is easiest to see on social media. Each time you are about to make a post or comment, ask yourself: *Is this necessary?* We live in an era, for the first time in human history, in which every random or fleeting thought, however immature or extraneous, can be announced, memorialized, and accessed forever on digital data bases. It is a disaster. Recent to this writing, a prominent editor was fired from a job for tweets made when she was a minor, and for which she had apologized in previous years. The permanency of consequence resulting from frivolity or bad choices online should never be underestimated.

It took me a long time to learn this lesson. I am still learning it. The lesson is difficult to abide because social media by its very structure encourages the dopamine rush of attention, the thrill of experiencing or engaging in confrontations (usually involving insulting or humiliating someone), the fear of exclusion—and, in sum, its use is addictive. And intentionally so. Hence, it is often overwhelmingly tempting to make a silly, sneering, or attention-seeking remark. The driving factor is that nearly everything on social media is a kind of contest.

And one comment can trigger that contest and enact time-wasting friction. Step out of it.

Likewise with talking. During the Covid lockdown "small talk" grew limited. Some people miss it. But watch carefully as it returns. In matters of necessity, you may or may not want to disclose your activities to someone with whom you are thrown into random contact on a car ride, dental visit, elevator, or flight. Many casual encounters center on complaining, which can be depleting. Sharing your ideas can also invite unwanted opinions, something that Napoleon Hill specifically warned of.

Necessity means practicing a degree of self-sufficiency. We often ask people to fetch things for us—"can you bring me the phone charger?"—which we can easily locate without burdening another. This type of behavior escalates in workplaces where some people seem to dedicate their entire jobs to making work for others. When I was in publishing, I once estimated that 20% of my workday was given to correcting mistakes or things that had been left incomplete, most times because someone didn't read through a set of instructions or bother to look at an explanatory note. Or simply didn't care. You may calculate a higher percentage in your own work life. I call this "task dumping": making work for another because of indifference to details. The practice of self-sufficiency also makes you a better colleague.

I have been inspired by spiritual teacher Vernon Howard (1918–1992). One night, Vernon told a roomful of students: *"All I'm really trying to say is, why don't you just leave people alone?"* He was exploring how we chronically invade other people's lives with extraneous comments, burdens, and frictions. Cleaving to necessity ameliorates that crisis—and in our digital era it gives you a way to stand taller. What you save in time, attention, and energy can be dedicated to more of what really matters to you.

In sum, when you abstain from the unnecessary you: 1) reduce possibilities for friction (especially on social media); 2) foster self-sufficiency; 3) avert the resentment of "task dumping" (which is an ethical violation of another's time); 4) experience the self-respect of carrying your own weight; and 5) preserve your attention and energy for tasks that truly matter. Eschewing the unnecessary virtually ensures your embrace of necessity—and the progress it brings.

Necessity is not necessarily the same as a crisis. But necessity escalated can indeed become one. Hence, we will revisit this point later when dealing with questions of emergencies or urgencies.

HABIT 4

Flexible Persistence

In sinologist John Blofeld's excellent 1968 translation of the ancient Chinese oracle the *I-Ching*, hexagram 36 reads: "Persistence amounting to madness should be avoided." How does one persist in the face of repeated difficulty and barriers without ceding to this trap?

This returns me to a morning recent to this writing. I had previously experienced a sleepless night filled with anxieties about work and career. Whatever our individual outlook or temperament, we all have such nights and I always promise never to conceal that kind of thing in my writing. When I awoke, I turned, seemingly at random, to a passage from *Think and Grow Rich* which lifted my emotions and settled my anxieties. It is about a "hidden Guide" who tests us. Napoleon Hill's observation from Chapter 9, "Persistence," reads:

> Sometimes it appears that there is a hidden Guide whose duty is to test men through all sorts of discouraging experiences. Those who pick themselves up after defeat and keep on trying, arrive; and the world cries, "Bravo! I knew you could do it!" The hidden Guide lets no one enjoy great achievement without passing the PERSISTENCE TEST. Those who can't take it, simply do not make the grade.
>
> Those who can "take it" are bountifully rewarded for their PERSISTENCE. They receive, as their compensation, whatever goal they are pursuing. That is not all! They receive something infinitely more important than material compensation—the knowledge that "EVERY FAILURE BRINGS WITH IT THE SEED OF AN EQUIVALENT ADVANTAGE."

Is this true? Is there a "hidden Guide?" Well, I can certainly tell you that the timing was propitious. More so, we all live by assumptions, whether spiritual, materialistic, or some variety. I suggest allowing your "maybe" to fall on the side of self-belief. Persistence and self-belief, when approached flexibly, can produce remarkable outcomes. One of the facets of flexible persistence is that the result can be fulfilling but also *surprising.*

I often say that when you are striving for something, of whatever nature, you should be very watchful for the arrival or fulfillment of your wish. Because, as explored next in Habit 5: *Harness Unexpected Forces*, your deliverance may, and often does, reach you in ways that are radically unexpected; or, by the same principle, *the solution may appear so routine that you are apt to overlook it.* I believe that we frequently dismiss opportunities—and even extraordinary events—because they do not reach us in the expected wrapping.

We are all creatures of prejudice. We want solutions that mirror preexisting beliefs, expectations, and self-perceptions. I once knew the author of a book on how to heal sinus infections naturally. His book had many thousands of grateful fans. He did excellent work and helped myriad people recover from chronic infections. But he confided to me that he once had a sinus infection and as much as he tried to employ his own methods—and had employed them successfully in the past—the thing just would not lift. He finally took antibiotics. He recovered. This does not mean his natural-health ideas were wrong or flawed. But the world is complex and we must sometimes bend with it.

Hence, your solution may reach you in novel or seemingly routine ways. Set a watcher at the gate and be vigilant. There are many ancient myths and parables where a god, mysterious messenger, or monarch is disguised as an ordinary traveler. Those who help him or display hospitality are showered with rewards. Metaphorically speaking, consider whether you are neglecting a mysterious messenger because he or she is clothed wrong. Be mindful of this. It could change everything for you.

I can only assume that my life is not exceptional or different in nature from anyone else's; so, I will share a personal experience from its arc. I am living out things today that I wished for at a very, very young age. There were many years of interruption. And there persist unfinished tasks. But I do take to heart something suggested by the philosopher and dramatist Johann Wolfgang von Goethe (1749–1832), which is that what we wish for when young visits us in waves when we are old. So be careful. Scan your earliest memories and judge the truth of that statement from your own perspective.

Now, there are unfinished desires, too—things that we yearn for like breath itself. What about those things? Well, let me offer a few observations. First, we sometimes focus on a thing that we cannot have—like an unrequited love interest. In some cases, I have found that a certain something—I cannot say what, but the experience was unmistakable—*protected* me from something

I wanted, like a job or an intimate relationship, only to receive something better and to later discover that the previous focus of my desire would have been depleting and possibly disastrous. Concentrate on what you want. Do not bargain anything away. *But always be ready for your desire to be fulfilled differently.* That is a vital part of the cosmic habit of flexible persistence.

Inasmuch as life visits tragedy on us, we sometimes encounter extraordinary and unexpected breakthroughs. In certain cases, an apparent or even painful loss is actually a victory, which takes time to be revealed as such. A spiritual organization once expelled me from its ranks. My spiritual search was considered too unorthodox. I was hurt but I stood by the validity of my search. That same organization was later engulfed in scandal and I was glad to be unattached to it. What had once seemed like an injury was more of a gift. There is healthful persistence in standing by one's beliefs.

No one questions that our behaviors and habits can contribute to catastrophe; but the same forces can likewise cultivate moments of profound breakthrough. One thing I have found is that persistence has remarkable delivering power. It is more often spoken of than exercised. I know few people who *truly* persist.

Persistence can, of course, be difficult to maintain. We sustain ourselves, however, by logging *interim victo-*

ries. In that vein, I want to share a quote that is often attributed to Goethe. You have probably seen it, or part of it, reproduced as a motivational or inspirational saying. But Goethe did not exactly write or utter it. It is a very loose rendering from the prelude of the dramatist's play *Faust* translated in 1835 by Irish poet John Anster. It goes like this:

> *Are you in earnest? Seize this very minute:*
> *What you can do, or dream you can, begin it;*
> *Boldness has genius, power, and magic in it.*
> *Only engage and then the mind grows heated;*
> *Begin and then the work will be completed.*

Although as reflective of the translator's outlook as Goethe's, I deem the passage true and I believe Goethe's work agreed with its general drift. It is the premise upon which this habit is based. If desire is truly present, then registering interim victories, based upon action, becomes a sustaining, grounding, and validating force. In order to avail ourselves of victory, however, we must have the flexibility to see it as a spectrum: victory gets reflected back to us in unexpected ways. And that is the step to which we now turn.

HABIT 5

Harness Unexpected Forces

I want to amplify a point made earlier. When seeking opportunities, rungs, or footholds, do not get excessively focused on the form in which they appear. We often persuade ourselves that the job, degree, relationship, or funding that we seek must arrive and look a certain way. But be extra watchful. As noted previously, the vessel or resource that you need often reaches you in a manner that differs from your mind's eye image. The mind seeks the familiar. But reality is diffuse.

"The things that are good for you," Napoleon Hill said in 1952, "the things that you desire most, begin to come back to you, and they come oftentimes from the most unexpected sources."

Indeed, life tends to bargain with you: you often receive some practical version of what you need—possibly exactly what you need or perhaps something better—but in a manner that presents itself through *expedient, sympathetic, or available means.* Hence, the delivery frequently differs from the nature of what you idealize. Do not permit that to deter you.

Some of the artists and creatives I most admire said "yes" at propitious moments and received resources vital to their work. Some specifically sought out resources by dedicating themselves to available and expedient vehicles, genres, or projects.

This process played out in the career of filmmaker George Romero (1940–2017) who is famous for *Night of the Living Dead, Dawn of the Dead,* and other zombie and horror movies. Romero is considered a horror visionary. He virtually created the zombie subgenre, which thematically abounds across movies, series, books, and videogames. The flesh-eating creature that Romero created or, some ways, recreated, is as recognizable as Dracula or the Frankenstein monster. Both of those creatures were themselves screen recreations of, respectively, an earlier corpus of folklore and Romantic novelist Mary Wollstonecraft Shelley's 1818 horror urtext. But Romero did not start out yearning to direct horror movies or to invent a new subgenre.

In the late 1960s, the Pittsburgh native was busy shooting local commercials and industrial films. Like many young directors, his eyes were on directing a feature movie. But the budding auteur said that he and his collaborators had no interest in making a horror film specifically. Indeed, Romero and his partners made a pragmatic decision to gravitate toward the genre simply due to the availability of investors and channels of distribution. It was a means for a capable filmmaker to break in.

"From *Night of the Living Dead*," the director told author Paul R. Gagne who documented Romero's career in his book *The Zombies That Ate Pittsburgh*, "I learned, most importantly, that people could do this . . . make movies . . . movies that looked and sounded like movies. That you didn't have to be born to it . . . that you didn't have to live in Hollywood."

Romero's gambit worked. Perhaps too well as the unsettling and innovative *Night of the Living Dead* eventually elevated him into a horror and even social icon. Although Romero ventured into other genres, his ability to attract investors and audiences returned him to horror for the rest of his career. In interviews, the director voiced some frustration about that. But he also became a legend. I consider it a valid bargain.

For similar reasons, another Pittsburgh native, novelist and screenwriter Jerry Stahl, collaborated with filmmaker Stephen Sayadian on the 1982 post-apocalyptic erotic classic *Café Flesh*. The artists, who met while working for Larry Flynt's *Hustler* magazine during its gonzo days in the mid-1970s in Columbus, Ohio, realized that the porn genre—although not known as an artistic boundary-buster—could grant them the freedom and funding to make an innovative film. Provided they covered certain requisites. In 2021, filmmaker Jacqueline Castel spoke to the movie's creators for her liner notes to a first-time release of the *Café Flesh* soundtrack by composer Mitchell Froom. The filmmaker described how the three subversives found within porn the creative vehicle that they needed:

> Sayadian was excited by the prospect of the genre's potential, and was granted an unusual level of creative freedom on his productions early on due to his off-kilter success at *Hustler*: "The opportunity in pornography was once you have sex, everything else was open," he said. "There's nothing you couldn't do" . . . Stahl said of breaking into pornographic pictures with Sayadian, "I would argue that it's less about the fact that it's pornography than I was working with a visionary artist," continuing, "the sex, to me, was almost the least innovative thing about it.

The fact that it was pornography was incidental. That was how we could get in the door. That's how we got a budget."

This kind of tactic does not always require pushing margins. Before dedicating myself fulltime to writing, I was the editor-in-chief of a metaphysical publishing imprint at Penguin Random House. I often encouraged the spiritual writers I published—many of whom were also friends—to say yes to basic, genre-driven non-fiction projects because such efforts provided them with the money and audience to pursue the esoteric ideas for which they felt passion. They could explore their ideas not in some watered-down, milquetoast way, but in a complete and robust way. Yet also with a framing that appealed to genre readers. This approach did not, of course, preclude their working on other, more esoterically themed works, some of which I also published. But category or genre publishing afforded these good authors practical and remunerative means of expression.

If you are interested in arcana, esoterica, meta-physics, or the occult, a basic "cookbook" on astrology, Tarot, meditation, or magick can grant you the vehicle to explore an extraordinary vista of topics, history, and themes. Indeed, I often advise budding writers with occult or paranormal interests to study newswriting.

Believe it or not, there actually are not enough good, workmanlike writers to cover the demand for basic, genre-driven titles in these areas. At least not when I was working on them. If you can write subject-verb-object sentences on Bigfoot, you will find readers. But few would-be writers invest the time to hone their craft. Many of the books I was proud to publish had the kind of basic genre appeal I am describing. For example, pick up Robert M. Place's *The Tarot*. Or Richard Smoley's *Supernatural*. Or Gary Lachman's *Aleister Crowley*. These accomplished artists did excellent work within— as well as beyond—genre parameters.

As a writer, I have attempted to act on my own advice. This book is a case in point. For me, the genres of self-help and practical spirituality are good vessels for exploring and applying esoteric and occult ideas. I did not always realize beforehand that I was couching esoteric ideas within mainline titles, themes, or structures. Indeed, some perceptive readers wrote to me to say that they detected what I was doing before I did.

I began my writing career as a historian of alternative spirituality. I call myself a "believing historian." I participate in the fields that I document, as do most historians of religion but often without saying so. I also write from the perspective of practical philosophy. In the book market, categories of self-help and practical spirituality are thriving and popular. They are evergreens. The market is well defined. Hence, by writing within these fields, I can integrally explore a landscape of subjects that are at once deeply meaningful to me and that reach a broad audience, something I also care about. My topics find expression within genres that are sufficiently commercial, yet also sufficiently flexible, so that I can succeed as a working author dedicated to metaphysical exploration.

Make no mistake: I live by every word I write. I am dedicated to sharing the facts of my search, and I never extend my word beyond it. But by writing, at least part of the time, within the vein of popular metaphysics and self-help—just as the previously mentioned creatives functioned within horror and porn—I have been able to produce a body of work that is, I hope, exploratory, adventurous, and, by measure of the market, sustainable.

If I insisted that a vessel conform in the strictest ways to my vision—and sometimes this occurs, too—I would potentially limit my ability to communicate with a wide range of readers. My dream of being a self-sustaining writer would be more distant. I ask you to consider how this principle can apply to your own life. This is part of what I mean when I counsel: *never neglect unexpected forces of fulfillment.*

Let me add a note to avert any misunderstanding. None of what I am saying involves "selling out," which

I define simply as putting money before quality. Nor does it mean reducing the maturity of your work. (Publishers err when they indirectly encourage "dumbing down" books. Readers are an exceptional minority. Respect them.) I am urging you to thoughtfully identify the vehicles that can convey your work. Never compromise core points or ideals. On that note, I am inspired by what novelist and capitalist philosopher Ayn Rand wrote in her 1962 essay, "Doesn't Life Require Compromise?":

> One cannot achieve the victory of one's ideas by helping to propagate their opposite. One cannot offer a literary masterpiece "when one has become rich and famous," to a following one has acquired by writing trash. If one found it difficult to maintain one's loyalty to one's own convictions at the start, a succession of betrayals—which helped to augment the power of the evil one lacked the courage to fight—will not make it easier at a later date, but will make it virtually impossible.

Part of this habit, as with the others in this book, derives from nature. Nature delivers resources efficiently. There are few indirect routes of arrival in nature—although there can be surprising ones. Trees appear on mountains not because seeds were rolled up hill but because birds in flight dropped seeds there. Water descends not rises, hence farms are often located on plains or lowlands. Accumulated frost and snow facilitate spring growth once rising temperatures allow for vegetation, flora, and crops. Life is sustained by symmetrical and symbiotic patterns. Watch for them. That is at the heart of Cosmic Habit Force. Ralph Waldo Emerson wrote in his essay "Fate" in 1860: "Nature is no spendthrift, but takes the shortest way to her ends."

Napoleon Hill put it this way in his 1952 talk on Cosmic Habit Force:

> Nature has definite ways of doing everything according to fixed habits that are inexorable and cannot be circumvented, cannot be avoided. And in the chemical actions of matter, from the smallest particle of matter, which is the electrons and the protons of the atom, to the largest particles of matter as they exist in the stars in the heavens, all actions and reactions of matter are based upon the fixed habits of Cosmic Habit Force. And in the perpetuation of every living thing through the sex principle, each seed reproduces its kind, but each individual reproduction is modified by the vibrations of the environment in which it exists.

These possibilities repeat within your personal sphere. The vessel that you seek, the funding that you need, the experience or education that you are pursuing, the relationship that you crave, personal or professional, will likely arrive through unexpected and even unsought channels or vehicles. Often these are innate to your environment. Cultivate awareness of them. When these channels, chariots, or vessels present themselves, take careful notice of their possibilities. If they fulfill what you need—even if that fulfillment differs from what you thought you were awaiting—*use them.*

I also want to note that when seeking the solution to a personal problem, no option should be off the table for you—including those options that our peer groups or cultural nests may not validate.

Orthodoxy does not belong to one side or another. It is a constant of human nature. Hence, one routinely encounters orthodoxies and prejudices within the alternative spiritual scene and its adjacent cultures. Things that are considered "mainstream"—such as money, pharmaceuticals, fashion, affluence, elective or cosmetic surgeries, consumer goods, pop culture, and so on—are sometimes regarded as symptoms versus solutions. But your associations with these things are highly individualized. And solutions can arrive from myriad sources, just as problems do.

I ask you to think really freely about what is right for you. With no one else's approbation. And without feeling bound by handed-down wisdom. Money cannot solve problems? It solves lots of problems. It may not always be available but that should not be conflated with its utility.

Often people who do not possess something expound on its limits. Or people who *do* possess something, and would not give it up for the world, talk about the emptiness of prizes, worldly goods, or personal attributes.

The point is not to favor one outlook or another—but to favor your own.

Even when using metaphysical approaches, in which I strongly believe, solutions may arrive through seemingly established, routine, or ordinary means. So much so that we might brush them aside. For example, who says a solution cannot arrive in the form of a pill? Why is that any less miraculous than any other approach?

I encounter people on social media, as I am sure you do, who hold calcified ideas about what constitutes "spirituality." Like any orthodox religionist, they might insist that "true principles" run along certain lines. People write things like, "The only way to know Truth is . . ." Fill in the blank with their experience. But we are interested here in *your* experience.

In spiritual circles we are sometimes told to verify things for ourselves. That principle must be meant seriously. It cannot mean, in effect, verify something and come back when what you have found matches what I already believe. Verify for yourself some solution that may not be supported by your subculture. Determine its value for you alone.

HABIT 6

Ever Higher

It is natural to get stuck in holding patterns. To slide into a groove with the same colleagues, clients, work-mates, efforts, and venues. But this will eventually sty-mie your energies and potential for growth. Sometimes aiming higher means *rejecting lower*. It means refusing events, jobs, and sources of income that, while possibly reassuring, dominate your time and energies in ways that subtly and gravitationally keep you in place among limiting colleagues and mediums.

It is an odd fact of human nature that new paths with-hold themselves until we develop the courage to dispense with old ones.

As I am writing these words in early 2021, I am struck by a symmetry that I detected almost by accident. Whenever I said "yes" to events that seemed questionable—perhaps to speaking engagements with venues that didn't have adequate budgets—more such events presented themselves. But when I refused events or media that my heart just was not in, either for the reasons I have just cited, or simply because the possibilities seemed shaky, newer and more significant offers flowed to me.

We cannot be certain of the basis of events. But it does seem clear that, since growth is continual, the holding open of a date or slot, bravely awaiting a truly meaningful opportunity rather than capitulating to a "safe" one, seems, in my experience, to result in progressively greater fulfillment. I often tell people that it is far better to be alone than to accept low company. If you hold out for the kinds of social engagements, relationships, or friendships that you truly want, you, in turn, stand taller, feel better about yourself, and thus become a more appealing and magnetic person who is likelier to attract needed things.

As I've written elsewhere, there are likely extraphysical qualities to communication—in *Think and Grow Rich*, Napoleon Hill describes a "sixth sense" as the thirteenth step to riches. In the decades since his book, academic study of anomalous transfer of information, or what is popularly called ESP, has statistically validated rather than disproven Hill's thesis. (I write further about this in Habit 22: *Expect Great Things*.) Surrounding debates are unlikely to be settled any time soon. But personally, I would not discount the prospect that when you opt for growth, your refusal of what you do not want is an emotionally and intellectually integral decision that may, in some manner that we do not fully understand, result in an act of communication or selection in the direction of what is desired.

When seeking to aim higher, you are not just metaphorically pulling yourself up a ladder, hoping that you will catch a new rung. That may be part of it. But an equal part, and, in some respects a potentially greater and self-determining part, is *refusing what you do not want*—which is almost always within your power to do. Releasing the familiar is frightening. And that is its value. Purposeful refusal is a bravely self-generated and unilateral step that you can take right now, or almost anytime, *to establish your set of standards*. Never do so frivolously. As just explored, vessels for opportunity can reach you in ways that differ from your idealized images. So, be practical. But, at the same time, honor the natural law that fills a channel when it becomes emptied.

There is a truism in real estate: You never want to own the nicest house on the block. If you do, it means that lesser properties can only drag your value down. Rather, you want to be in a position of benefiting from the worth of the surrounding properties. A similar dynamic can be applied to your work and business relationships. As my partner Jacqueline Castel, a film-maker, put it to me: "You want to be the least-talented person on a project." You benefit from collaborators, investors, and coworkers who surpass and intrinsically elevate you; who demand more of you; who improve your best.

I have had to learn this lesson the hard way—perhaps you have, too. Have you ever had the experience of sitting in a meeting or on a Zoom call and realizing with a sinking feeling in your stomach that you are listening to a string of mediocre or off-kilter ideas? When I worked in publishing, I would sometimes encounter a prejudice against dedicating marketing and publicity resources to certain kinds of books—usually reissues, translations, or anthologies: books that were not considered the right profile for publicity. But if such books are selling well—and possibly outselling their more conventional counterparts—how does it serve the catalogue (or the company's owners or investors) not to dedicate resources to them?

For example, I once published a new translation of the meditations of Marcus Aurelius. It proved surprisingly commercial. Bookstores in the California Bay

Area began to request appearances and signings by the co-translator, a well-known philosopher who lived in Oakland. I brought this good news to a senior colleague in publicity. She looked confused and replied, "Well, we don't usually arrange signings for that kind of book . . ." Her voice trailed off. At the same time, publicity resources were being dedicated to a nonfiction wilderness survival narrative. It was a worthy book; but it did not sell as well. Regardless, significant sums were dedicated to it and none to the more successful translation; this was due to perception. The philosopher was left to make bookstore arrangements on his own with no support. His book continues to sell today. This upside-down logic told me that I was always not dealing with colleagues who could uplift me. I was sometimes in the position of trying to pull them up rather than be improved myself. This is the kind of position that you do not want to linger in.

Aiming higher means seeking colleagues who outperform you. Who give you a raised bar for which to aspire. And who can collaboratively correct your shortcomings rather than leaving you to (often vainly) attempt to correct theirs, which generally results in resentment and futility rather than real improvement. In fact, most people do not want to improve. They want to determine who within an organization or partnership dispenses favors and money and then please that

person (who may also be on their own level of talent)—
not to strengthen their output.

Some of the biggest mistakes I have made in life
involved settling for safe or so-so collaborators. Whenever possible, seek collaborators, bosses, financiers,
and coworkers with whom you must strive to keep up.
Again, we are often lured into second-rate relationships
by fear. We may appreciate the attention or willingness
of certain people to aid us and, hence, we consent to
work with them because *we are unsure whether other
and possibly better alternatives will appear.* Attention and
enthusiasm are extremely important. But they can peter
out. They are not a substitute for aligning yourself with
the highest possible collaborators.

A similar dynamic appears in personal relationships.
I have witnessed more good people harm themselves
by remaining in *depleting intimate relationships* than
any other single factor. It is a common human trait—
including among highly effective men and women—to
fear loss or loneliness so acutely that they settle for
poor company or even emotionally abusive partners or
friends. (I return to the topic of avoiding emotional pre-
dation in Habit 20.)

Life is complex and, as such, I try not to state things
in absolutist terms—but years of observation and experience have given me full confidence in the statement

I made earlier: *It is vastly better to be nobly alone than to compromise with low company.* As alluded, you will not only stand taller but you will, as an outgrowth of high standards of self-respect, attract better and more sympathetic partners. Whether in terms of friends or a love interest, jettisoning deteriorative relations all-but-guarantees proximity to more satisfying people.

This revolutionizing decision or habit rests wholly in your hands. Or it almost always does. But you must be inwardly honest about what you really want. Do you really want healthful friendships or relationships? We often grow attached to inappropriate people because we undervalue ourselves. Or we seek out the comfort of the familiar even when it is painful. The unhappy familiar provides a cold though seemingly stable compact. Or we secretly doubt our ability to attract and sustain fuller relationships. For these reasons, we may undermine *what we say we want* in relationships or collaborations. Aiming higher must be a true wish and determined decision, whether in matters of work or intimacy.

It must be acknowledged that aiming higher sometimes brings rejection, which is why we avoid it. I believe that we spend too much time fearing rejection or attempting to salve our wounds by explaining it away. I am guilty of this myself. But we can never fully understand another's reasons for rejection. It is highly subjective and emotionally keyed. We fear the hurt that rejection brings—yet fear of rejection is the primary thing that binds us to outmoded and unproductive circumstances.

And consider: is rejection really so bad? Rejection is often just circumstantial. Another person or organization may need or understand what you are offering at a given moment. It is largely based on perception. I have personally witnessed rejection morph into pursuit when the previously rejecting party came to fear that they were "missing out." (In the world of media acquisitions, "missing out" is the ultimate sin.) A successful publisher told me, "I never take 'no' as a final answer. Because conditions change and then the answer changes."

All of us project our insecurities onto whatever we believe we cannot have. In this way, the emotional pain of rejection is often *self-created*. It is also overinflated. Indeed, we are more apt to dwell on rejection than on acceptance. This is because sharper emotions are involved, particularly the fear intrinsic to our private sense of unworthiness. When a person, group, or business rejects us, it makes that party seem all the more important or alluring simply because the rejection taps our self-doubt. (Beware that this does not get used on you as a tool of manipulation, something explored in Habit 20: *Avoid Predatory Personalities*.)

So, understand that any reach for a new rung will inevitably lead to occasional rejection or misses. That is a given. But you must not permit the fear of rejection—which is often an emotional construct—to cement you into low circumstances. That amounts to self-establishing what you fear. Begin to understand rejection less as an outer event and more as your *personal reaction*, which, based on what we have just explored, it is. Pain from rejection will more quickly dissipate and become emotionally forgotten as you experience the progressing benefits of aiming higher.

Ever higher is the one certain means of avoiding out-moded company, a principle on which we expand next in Habit 7: *The Law of Proximity*. Entering healthfully challenging or higher relationships advances your cause and self.

HABIT 7

The Law of Proximity

"The very moment I come into contact with any person who has a bad influence on me," Napoleon Hill said in an unpublished lecture, "I immediately disassociate myself from that person. I don't care who it is. It might even be my mother-in-law or a close relative. And oftentimes, believe you me, I have had to disassociate myself from close relatives." I applaud his bluntness.

It is critical that you seek company, personally and professionally, that reflects who and where you wish to be. Never settle for contact, either professionally, intimately, or socially, with people whose ethics, conduct, choices, and intellectual prowess do not reflect your aspirations.

As you can see from Hill's statement, this principle should be interpreted in the strictest and most liberating sense. No one can ultimately force you to settle for low company. The consequences may be difficult to bear—in some cases you may deem the consequences too difficult, especially when economic need is involved—but never neglect the liberating possibility that this ideal suggests. Indeed, if you encounter a circumstance where you feel you cannot sever withering ties, examine the matter carefully—ensure that the ties are as imperative as you believe. Often, they are not. Or if they are, the imperative may be situational or temporary. It may have a time limit.

In seeking fortifying relations, and in rejecting depleting ones, I want to add an important caveat. I am not talking about social climbing or restricting your relationships to people who are "useful." I have witnessed such approaches and they are often transparent. They may net some gains, but they come with the inner cost of self-degradation, which results in unhappiness and anxiety. You will never respect yourself unless you are able to function among myriad groups of people. And you will need the help of a wide range of people, including those in the trades, professions, or no particular field at all, who possess intellect, real-world wisdom, and reliability. So, bear in mind that I am not talking about restricting your social circle to people who occupy whatever professional rung you perceive as above your own, but rather about drawing a circle that includes only those people who demonstrate ability, intellect, and steadiness. Or other factors you admire and toward which you aspire. These may include traits in which you feel deficient. Emulate and do not resent their exemplifiers.

The motivational writer Anthony Norvell (1908–1990) wrote about the "law of proximity" in his 1963 book, *The Million Dollar Secret Hidden In Your Mind*. Norvell counseled that before you admit someone to your life on a serious, personal basis you should ask:

- Will our friendship by mutually good?
- What do I have to offer this person and what does he have to give?
- Does he have habits that are negative and that might impede my course in life?
- Are his standards high?
- Have I got anything to learn from my association with this friend?

It is, of course, necessary to cultivate transactional professional relationships. Every salesperson, investor, entrepreneur, grant writer, and artist knows that more business gets done, and more projects get funded, over personal relationships that any other single factor. Yes, excellence matters; return on investment matters. But most of the time *people fund those who they know, like, and trust.* In politics and the arts, the people I know who have most fully succeeded have spent significant amounts of their time seeking the company of supporters. This is not always easy. It may mean hanging around social circuits—including receptions, parties, bars, and restaurants—when you would rather be home in your socks watching a movie. But it is a tough truth of life (and one that I do not always abide by myself) that cultivating relationships is the most effective means of business transaction. If this requirement is off-putting then consider your career choice.

There is also a concrete benefit to circulating among large groups of people. Coincidence favors those who get noticed. In his 1986 book *How to Get Lucky*, journalist Max Gunther considered the careers of actors Kirk Douglas (1916–2020) and Lauren Bacall (1924–2014), both of whom were trying to break through in New York City in the late 1930s and early 1940s. Both were friends. Bacall, though younger, succeeded first and assisted Douglas. They both had a shared habit, which, in turn, led them to know each another. They were inveterate "connectors"—they got to know everyone. Gunther observes that Douglass

... got himself involved in a whirl of people and events. One person he got to know was a young would-be actress named Lauren Bacall.

At the time, it seems highly unlikely that this unknown young woman in bargain basement clothes could ever be the conduit of special luck for him. She had no power or contacts in high places. If Kirk Douglas had engineered his social life with the cynical goal of meeting the rich and powerful, he would have ignored this Lauren Bacall. But so cynical and narrow-focused an approach isn't likely to produce good luck. The lucky personality gets to know everybody in sight: the rich and the poor, the famous and the humble, the sociable and even the friendless and the cranky ... It is in the nature of luck to bring about fast, profound, unforeseen changes in situations—also in people.

Note that these performers did not limit themselves to the obvious sources of benefit. Star-coddling can seem like an evident source of benefit but hidden consequences abound. I know from an eyewitnesses that years ago a noted psychology professor at an Ivy League university upbraided a departmental secretary for belatedly giving him a phone message from a celebrity powerhouse with whom the professor had collaborated. The professor was eager to accommodate this major star. He valued his public association with him. The celebrity? Bill Cosby. The very rung that we think will support our weight can snap beneath our feet. Never persuade yourself that kissing up to a VIP or influencer is a sound or ethical plan, at least in the long run.

There is further potential for the law of proximity to be used in the negative. Some people within corporate structures become ruthlessly adept at misusing the law of proximity: they deliver mediocre work but keep their jobs because they learn *how to serve the bureaucracy.* I have known people in media companies who (perhaps unconsciously) perceived themselves as working not for the audience, investors, or artists—but strictly for the internal bureaucracy and its managers. In truth, this is sometimes a workable formula for retaining your job. It is also, and more unfailingly, a formula for listless output; disservice to customers, backers, and colleagues; and evasion of responsibility. If the work-for-the-bureaucracy approach brings you temporary job security, it also comes with self-abnegation.

In sum, the true meaning of the law of proximity appears in a maxim by Scottish-American philosopher Thomas Davidson (1840–1900). William James quoted it in an elegy to Davidson in 1905: "Associate with the noblest people you can find; read the best books; live with the mighty. But learn to be happy alone."

HABIT 8

Loosen the Hold of Fear

"Cosmic Habit Force is synonymous with the great River of Life," Napoleon Hill wrote in *The Master Key to Riches*, ". . . for it consists of a negative and a positive potentiality, as do all forms of energy." In that vein, we can get lost in habits that are destructive as easily as their opposite. Among the worst of these habits, often as devastating as substance addiction, is the *habit of fear*. It requires special consideration.

Hill described the problem of fear this way in 1952:

> If you're going to make the most out of the great thing that was given you at birth, the right to

control your own mind, you've got to learn that wherever fear appears, there's something in your makeup that needs to be corrected. And fear is something like physical pain: it's an indication that there is a cause that needs to be removed. You know, the most marvelous device of nature, perhaps of all other things, is the device of physical pain. It's the one universal language through which nature speaks to every living creature, and which every living creature respects. And when you are suffering mental pain through any form of fear, it means there is something in your character, something in your makeup that you have allowed to get in there that needs to be interpreted and removed. And those fears are not going to remove themselves, ladies and gentlemen. You've got to remove them. You've got to find the cause; you've got to work out a plan for eliminating that cause, whatever it may be.

In working out such a plan, it is imperative to acknowledge that fear, like low company, can take on a pleasurable or safely familiar dimension even as the experience is ostensibly painful. I have struggled much of my life with fear. For me, fear is often a kind of *reassurance that I am being vigilant.* Ironically, fear brings me a sense of safety—as though I am "keeping watch."

Indeed, when I was younger, I believed that letting go of fear, or even trying to, would place me at risk. It meant lowering my guard. This is one of the ways that fear becomes self-reinforcing. Fear disguises itself as protection.

I came to realize later in life, however, that, absent matters of physical safety, fear played almost no productive role in my professional existence. Slowly, I gave up seeing fear as a source of protection. Instead, I came to realize that my wellbeing, creatively, interpersonally, and economically, rests on three factors:

1. My desire for attainment. Some may describe this as a variant of fear. But I dissent from that. I think generativity, productivity, and creativity are at the heart of our existence.

2. My awareness of financial responsibility, budgeting, and scheduling. I know what I owe to finance, debt, and commerce. I understand my needs and my obligation to them.

3. Reciprocity to collaborators and contractors. Keeping my word in matters of deadline, delivery, and completion is a key ethic. Ayn Rand called it the "sanctity of contract." It presents a more positive source of guidance than fear.

It struck me: with these factors as companions, *fear is superfluous*, at least from a logical perspective. Outside matters of safety, fear rarely adds anything of constructive use or insight to a situation. Fear is more likely to becloud than to clarify. And fear causes all the familiar emotional-physical maladies, from sleeplessness to the risk of stress-related illnesses.

That said, it is very difficult, if not impossible, to persuade myself *by intellect alone* not to experience fear. Fear plays upon our minds, bodies, and emotions. It is important to keep in mind that all these different forces are at work in us independently. The intellect says, "I will not get angry," or some such, but the emotions have their own life and anger flares up anyway. Likewise, the body goes its own way: certain stresses begin in the body and they are as difficult to control (I might even say impossible) as runaway emotions.

So, first and foremost do not feel burdened that your thoughts have some *obligation* to control your anxieties. At the same time, there are some valuable exercises to attempt. They are based on esoteric philosophy but I believe you will find them very practical.

1. When you feel anxiety welling up in your emotions or body, you can talk in a friendly, relatable way to your emotional center and your body and say, in effect, "We are all on the same side here. We need

a good night's sleep. We need to do our work. If you're upset about something, I promise that I'll try to resolve it—but let's all work together." I think there exists a different quality of self—I call it the Nameless Self—that exists apart from the intellect, emotions, and body. That Nameless Self, or if you like call it your psyche (some might say your soul), is the being doing the talking. Talk aloud if it helps. Or silently. See if you get a response in the form of relaxation.

2. Repetition has its place. I believe that even if you cannot enter the "feeling state" of your goal you can nonetheless repeat affirmations. And this is more than just a mechanical act. I believe that the practice of affirmation, although a conscious, mental performance, can eventually and across time influence your self-perception. One victory in repeating an affirmation and feeling a greater sense of self-possession or witnessing an aim-come-true can be hugely fortifying.

3. There is a special energy in group activities. As some readers know, I enter into a short period of silent intention—a long-distance "Miracle Club"—each day at 3 p.m. eastern. Join me whenever you like: every day, intermittently, or just once. At that hour,

I think of every one of us who is working together, and I hold a wish for your power, honor, and highest intentions. No matter what else is going on, barring a medical emergency, I am in silent thought-intention-prayer at that time daily. The more of us who do this together, the more power we have, a theme to which I return in Habit 15: *Cultivate Inner Power*.

4. Finally, I always recommend some form of meditation as a method for disrupting calcified patterns. I personally practice Transcendental Meditation (TM). You can learn about TM online through the David Lynch Foundation.

I must add a further observation regarding fear and money. The role of fear in personal finance requires special amplification and exploration. Many of us grew up with—and are controlled by—fearful attitudes around money. This is natural. No human quality other than sexuality is invested with greater emotional complexity than money. That is why we are often prone to irrational actions around money, including chronic debt spending or the breaking of family ties and relationships over financial disputes.

Emotion rules money. That is a core truth of life. As such, fear often rules us in money management, earnings, debt, and a sense of financial security. This clouds decision-making and can even spoil a person's enthusiasm for life. I write those words from experience. I grew up in a childhood home wracked by financial crisis and it marked me always.

Yet in adulthood I also came to realize that fear—unless it signals a legitimate need for safety—rarely produces sound judgment relating to money or anything else. Fear is probably the greatest barrier to your capacity for constructive action. Indeed, procrastination itself is a type of fear and may be the most common (and overlooked) form that fear takes. We grow only when challenged; but we cannot grow if fear overwhelms us.

In that vein, I am providing an adaptation of Napoleon Hill's immensely important advice on fear from *Think and Grow Rich*. Whenever you feel plagued by fear, including in the middle of the night or the early hours of the morning when you should be sleeping, I want you to reflect on this short passage. There may be times when I am doing it with you. The words that you are about to read are the truth. Allow them to act as a beacon to guide you through the corridors of fear. If you find this passage useful, write it down, hang it up someplace you can see it—and share it.

Fear should never be bargained with or capitulated to. It takes the appeal from your personality, destroys the possibility of accurate thinking, diverts concentration of effort, stifles persistence, turns your willpower into nothingness, erases ambition, clouds your memory, and invites failure in every conceivable form.

Fear kills love, assassinates the finer emotions of the heart, discourages friendship, and leads to sleeplessness, misery, and unhappiness.

So pernicious and destructive is the emotion of fear that it is, almost literally, worse than anything that can befall you.

If you suffer from a fear of poverty, reach a decision to get along with whatever wealth you can accumulate WITHOUT WORRY. If you fear the loss of love, reach a decision to get along without love, if that becomes necessary. If you experience a general sense of worry, reach a blanket decision that *nothing that life has to offer is worth the price of fear.* This places Ultimate Truth at your back.

And remember: The greatest of all remedies for fear is a BURNING DESIRE FOR ACHIEVEMENT, backed by useful action in pursuit of your aim.

HABIT 9

Weigh the Cost of Suffering

In an unpublished talk, Napoleon Hill cautioned: "Avoid persons and circumstances which make you feel inferior."

Consider how rarely we heed such advice. And how often we involve ourselves in social-media chains or postings, relationships, activities, and entertainment that makes us feel deficient, angry, or inferior. There is a kind of prurient thrill in it: we get angry, we complain, we vent, and we repeat the cycle again. Be very watchful for the *pleasure* or satisfaction that you experience from negative emotions and entanglements—the false sense of excitement that such things may bring—and consider what this cycle costs you.

The previous cosmic habit was specifically about releasing fear. Let's revisit that for a moment. Now, ostensibly, I do not enjoy feeling afraid. And yet . . . even though the effects of fear may include pain, the emotion itself—like anger, aggression, truculence, intimidation, or cries of victimhood—delivers a kind of prurient thrill. It provides relief from the routine hours of life. It provides a feeling that I am at the center of attention. It provides a sense of challenge or contest.

Why else would we persist in clearly hurtful patterns?

As noted, there is a reassuring quality to familiarity, even in painful family dynamics. I have heard the term "trauma bonding." I honor that insight. But my proposition is based on slightly different premises.

Spiritual teacher Vernon Howard once asked students to write on a slip of paper the phrase "false feeling of life"—and then study it for six months. We all crave reward, excitement, and thrill. But we often conceal from ourselves *the self-negating manner by which we seek it.*

The yearning for thrill—so evident from gladiatorial events in the ancient world and violent sports media and gaming today (and much else)—is a near-constant of human nature. Watch carefully for whether you gain a sense of contest, aliveness, and thrill, through self-sought conflict, anger, or suffering.

It is not always easy for me to observe this pattern in my own life. But my contention—and I am working on this with you as I write these words—is that *what is found is generally what is sought.* This is true even when the thing sought reaches us in a form that we complain about. Sometimes complaining *is* the point. We bond through complaints; we get others to listen to us. Watch for whether your burdens are self-selected as the quickest means to attention, relationship, thrills, contest, relief of boredom, or some other payoff.

We all witness self-fulfilling prophecies in which we or others trigger the thing that is most feared. But why? *Why should fear alone produce an event?* Do we psychically "attract" it? Do we precognitively sense it?* Or something else? As I pondered the nature of self-fulfilling prophecies it came to me that, again and again, the decisive factor is *overcompensation.* Overcompensation is one of our greatest adversaries. Fear of rejection, for example, may result in forcing yourself on someone, which inevitably produces rejection. We overcompensate for perceived flaws. And, hence, we bring those

---

* This is more than supposition. E.g., see "Intuition Through Time: What Does the Seer See?" by Dean Radin, Ph.D., and Ana Borges, J.D., *Explore*, 2009; Vol 5, No. 4, 200–211.

flaws, phantom or not, to the pinnacle of our lives. It is a strange symmetry. But unrealized power dwells within that symmetry provided we can become aware of it. If events are self-created, then they can be self-altered.

I have always been fascinated with the myth of Oedipus and how he self-fulfilled the prophecy that he would kill his father and wed his mother. In the events of the Sophocles play *Oedipus Rex*, the tragic hero—powerful in intellect but vulnerable in pride and easily provoked to anger—is so fearful of this prophecy that he triggers it through a series of rash behaviors. The fear of an outcome, when extreme, engenders behaviors that are intended as medicine but instead are poison. It has been observed that medicine and poison are the same, depending upon dose.

Hence, someone who fears exclusion, either in business, friendship, or intimacy, often copes with that fear by acting out in ways that make his or her exclusion a fact. There may, on occasion, be a kernel of truth to our fears. But exaggeration or lack of self-awareness make that kernel a much greater factor than is necessary. Overcompensation also blinds us—Oedipus ultimately suffered blindness—so that we fail to detect the opportunity to bypass the wrong situation or company in favor of something more promising.

To cite a small but vivid example, I watched this play out in a mini psychodrama at a party one night. An out-of-town guest was eager to be seen and heard. He kept insistently butting into conversations or interrupting people. He wanted their acceptance, company, and recognition. But his anxiety to be seen made the people whose attention he sought distance themselves. It was a template of what I am describing.

Ask yourself today: What am I summoning? Do I really want it? And, if so, why? If not, why not? Pay less attention, for now, to the motive behind your desire than to what your desire is delivering.

And if the event, or more likely the pattern of events, causes you pain, is it actually a misdirected search for selfhood and power? Again: we often receive what we seek. What is sought may cause suffering but it also delivers something, albeit through a self-negating form of attention or the uneasy relief of self-compelled failure. We sometimes impel failure to cope with its perceived inevitability. Watch carefully for these factors.

The point of this habit, this awareness, is to seek positive attention, not negative attention. Seek positive power through self-development, not negative power through insistent appeals. Seek self-direction rather than self-abnegation, especially in relations with others. This theme continues in our next habit: constructive relating or, more specifically: how snark weakens you.

HABIT 10

Snark Weakens You

Napoleon Hill often wrote about the need for "tolerance"—of abiding different views, positions, and so on. In our digital age, often marked by an all-knowing cynicism, this kind of principle can seem toothless, sentimental, or irrelevant. Coarseness, insult, goading, pettiness, rhetorical questioning, and, above all, sarcasm dominate our digital age, which is to say: our lives.

"Do you recognize," Hill asked his Success Unlimited club, "... that you can't just leave yourself wide open to all of the remarks, to all of the influences, to all of the negative thoughts that are being broadcast through the ether at all times?"

Today that "ether" is social media. It is where we spend most of our professional, recreational, conversational, and even intimate hours. In aggregate, we spend far more time in cyberspace than we do with friends, loved ones, and even adversaries. Indeed, the sense of consequence-free behavior that pervades social media—a false sense, as many learn—intensifies the disinhibition we feel about lobbing verbal grenades, something that we would rarely be foolish enough (the word brave hardly seems to apply) to do in outer life.

Unless some genuine or consequential misunderstanding is at stake, I will not respond to sarcastic comments or rhetorical questions on social media. That is not my sole category for nonresponse, but it is the most important, and I recommend it. (I also try to avoid going over things that are already explored in my books or articles; although for earnest questions I make exceptions.)

Much of what fuels social-media posts are not social or political points but *conflicts of will*—someone makes a smartass remark, another commentator one-ups it, and the chain virally multiplies. Conflicts of this type are, as a rule, a waste of your time, energy, and resources. They are often acts of avoidance that detain us from necessary work and relationships. Watch carefully for the emotional pull such conflicts have on you.

The impulse to dominate or one-up an interlocutor feeds millions of social-media chains. It reflects the monetization of anger on a scale never before experienced. This compulsion preys upon another malady of human nature, which is the need for, almost the obsession with, expressing negative impulses toward another person. We believe that airing complaints or diminishing other people will dilute, and thus ease, whatever private tensions or doubts we feel. This is a false bargain. In fact, snark and smears, while delivering a momentary high, make you feel worse because the false cure fails, and you have adopted the burden of reciprocity for your disdain or vitriol, which is often experienced as shame. Or, to view it differently, the false cure is *shame deflected*. To protect ourselves from feelings of shame or failure, we dive into another pixilated fight, perhaps scoring yet another fleeting but futile thrill.

By contrast, every time that you abstain from a gratuitous remark, either spoken or posted, you grow subtly and authentically stronger. You can witness this process in yourself almost immediately. Next time you encounter the opportunity to be a smartass and *do not take it*, you will feel yourself grow more fibrous. Test this.

I am amazed by the number of people who never realize that silence is an actual option. Many of us are subtly conditioned to believe that silence is unnatural, either in person or online. We often encourage young children to talk for no reason whatever. We frequently regard quiet people, or people who just happen to be quiet at a given moment, as harboring offense or needing to be cajoled into whatever louder activity—either talk or noise—is occurring.

At many colleges, students are, in ways large and small, encouraged or even rewarded for sharing whatever attitude, outlook, or sentiment they feel, even if it is accompanied by limited experience with the issue at hand. As alluded, the online economy monetizes and exacerbates these tendencies by providing endless, and often feckless, opportunities for—the term scarcely seems appropriate—*sharing*. Often over the most frivolous things. Indeed, most sharing, in this context, is complaining. The definition of complaining is not exactly opposition or negativity; it is deriving a sense of self from the voicing of every discomforted emotion.

Now, to engage constructively does *not* have to mean saying something nice or anodyne. It means evaluating what to express on the *scale of necessity*, as explored in Habit 3. It also means that not every private dislike requires airing or at least not airing in a vituperative manner. Watch what occurs online when the name of any controversial author or topic arises. You often witness a feeding frenzy of assaultive responses, as if no quarter can be granted to a reference outside of exactly what one wants to hear.

Years ago on a train, I saw a dreadlocked back-packer—a young woman, maybe age 19 or 20—pull out a worn paperback of *Atlas Shrugged* by radical capitalist philosopher Ayn Rand. I could see that she was deep into reading it. I have no idea what value, if any, the backpacker found in the book, which tends to ignite polarized reactions. But I was struck at that moment that, granted the opportunity, I would never want to do anything to disparage or limit in another person the same unimpeded search that I wish for myself.

Although this episode occurred before the digital age, I hope that I have carried its impression with me. The episode left me with two ground rules by which I attempt to live and on which I close this chapter:

1. *Never shame authentic query.*
2. *Authentic query does not require an enemy.*

HABIT 11

Telling the Truth, or The Deity of Reciprocity

Reciprocity is the silent arbiter that enforces truth-telling. Or redresses its opposite. I do not believe that our era is any less honest than previous ones. But never has humanity possessed such a diversity of methods to violate truth.

In his 1870 collection *Society and Solitude*, Ralph Waldo Emerson wrote in the essay "Success" about the crisis of veracity:

I hate this shallow Americanism which hopes to get rich by credit, to get knowledge by raps on midnight tables, to learn the economy of the mind by phrenology, or skill without study, or mastery without apprenticeship, or the sale of goods through pretending that they sell, or power through making believe you are powerful, or through a packed jury or caucus, bribery and "repeating" votes, or wealth by fraud. They think they have got it, but they have got something else,—a crime which calls for another crime . . . We countenance each other in this life of show, puffing, advertisement and manufacture of public opinion; and excellence is lost sight of in the hunger for sudden performance and praise.

I am nearly at a loss as to what could be added to that, but Emerson's statement warrants special attention in our social-media era when people routinely purchase followers, sell tweets, covertly advertise goods, create fake accounts, and buy placement in feeds. Since this book is based on the ideas of Napoleon Hill, I should also add that Hill called Ralph Waldo Emerson a hero. Hence, I think that reading Hill and Emerson together is a good exercise: Emerson provides the necessary ethical teeth to Hill's outlook.

Before continuing the theme of reciprocity, I want to explore some of the commercial and interpersonal complexities of our present moment. Social media is, to a significant degree, a gamed system where selling is done under the cloak of "sharing." From my publishing days, I have personally seen pricelists where professional athletes or celebrities are paid through marketing agencies to tweet about products without any indication to followers that the post is a for-profit, unlabeled ad. In most cases, the celebrity or athlete has probably not heard of the product. Ka-ching. In ways small and large, many of us buy into this model of legalized fraud in which "influencers"—their means, methods, and sources of income concealed—persuade us of commercial claims. You can see why Emerson was adamant about the flimflam of his era. What does his statement say about ours?

Subterfuge is so common in digital retail and media that it is difficult to realize its pervasiveness. Duplicity is a distressingly common feature of interpersonal business, as well. Most of the time it never gets caught. But, again, there is a price. The perpetrator silently adopts the mantle of liar, which follows him or her into private life, quietly and unseen, but with subtle and cumulative consequences.

It is impossible to compartmentalize one's behavior, any more than to divide the elements that compose water and still have the same substance. Life is sticky. It is whole. *You are who you are wherever you are.* Mislead a customer, client, collaborator, or social media follower and sooner than you know, you will mislead a loved one. Or you will be misled. It is that stark. And keep in mind that personal behavior is rarely conditioned by circum-stance. A thief is a thief in both good times and bad. An honest person is generally always honest—not just when it is advantageous. Or that person is, by defini-tion, dishonest. Human nature is consistent.

Truth-telling is vital for the human economy. Truth itself forms a special currency—it may be the ultimate currency. As the global economy grows increasingly dig-itized and businesses morph into "platforms" for selling third-party goods rather than as outlets of production, truth may become the most precious commodity on earth. But truth is more than that.

Truth and veracity are the binding agents of life. Whether you can trust someone determines who you conduct business with; whose word you accept; how you relate to your friends, neighbors, coworkers, col-laborators, and family members; and, ultimately, who you plan to spend your life with. In short, truth, or your perception of it, determines who you allow in and who you exclude. Truth is the invisible tie—or, when absent, fissure—that shapes your life. That is why it is so grave a matter when truth gets violated.

And, unfortunately, truth gets violated all the time—not always at moments of schismatic or private conflict but also in routine matters, touching on rela-tions in your workplace, who you enter contracts with, whose medical advice you take, and who you hire or are hired by. We do not often notice or acknowledge violations of truth until after the fact. If you are like me, you may even *deny* that you were misled. It hurts too much. Abuse of truth sometimes occurs in ways that you simply do not wish to acknowledge.

As I write these words, I am reminded of a situation where I was misled in a manner that came to light without ambiguity. Several years ago, I was in the running to narrate the audio edition of a book that was being made into a movie. I was a longtime fan of the book, a friend of its author, and, as a frequent audiobook narrator, I was eager and hopeful to land the job. Yet the supervising producer, who I had never met, seemed arbitrarily opposed to my participation. She emailed me to say that the author did not want me to narrate the book. She was unaware that he and I were friends. I approached him about it and he said that what I had been told was untrue; in fact, he shared an email that contradicted what the producer said. A friend consoled me: "It's a lie, but it's just a business lie." Well, I am not sure there is any such thing. The claim that "it's just business" has always struck me as meaningless if not obfuscatory. Again: life is whole. Truth binds it. Truth is either present or absent.

As suggested by the title of this chapter, my story had a positive resolution. Although the producer shut

me out, the movie flopped (which I note without satisfaction), and I soon narrated another, truly iconic
historical work for the same audio publisher. In the second case, the author handpicked me following a round
of auditions. The process was transparent. The project
itself was hugely satisfying. It is among the narrations of
which I am personally proudest. Ironically, or perhaps
meaningfully, I would not have been in the running for
the second job had I gotten the first since the two projects were produced back-to-back. In short, the violation
of truth delivered me to a better result.

What I have just described is one of the strange
workings of reciprocity, sometimes called karma or
compensation. Under any name, this concept suggests
that, ultimately, no truth or plain dealing can be violated, at least not permanently. We may not always see
the pendulum swing that adjusts a violation. It is not
always granted to us, either in time or perspective, to
witness a natural course correction. But nature tends
toward stability and stasis. I believe this applies to
events, personalities, and relationships, just as it does
to the natural world.

This may be the dynamic that Nietzsche had in
mind when he wrote in *Beyond Good and Evil* in 1886:
"One *has* to repay good and ill—but why precisely to the
person who has done us good or ill?" (Again, from the
Kaufmann translation.) In this maxim, Nietzsche takes

an impersonal view of life, probably close in nature to Vedic theology. I might frame it that "nature *has* to repay" rather than "one *has* to repay." The scales of equilibrium are, within traditional Hinduism and Buddhism, unseeable and ineffable, not infrequently harsh, and spread across vast spans of time. But I cannot, of course, discount that Nietzsche specifically addresses himself to the individual. We often hear the concept of "pay it forward" when we receive a benefit. But can—*should*—that concept also be applied to life's injustices? I am uncomfortable with that prospect since it borders on spite. At the same time, Nietzsche's statement may reflect modes of behavior in which we engage all the time. It is for the seeker to determine the ultimate application.

I believe that we live, effectively or literally, under a "deity of reciprocity," to borrow a term from the brilliant 2019 folk horror movie *Midsommar*.* Its workings are detectable across life.

Indeed, cycles of reciprocity rewarded me in connection with the words that you are now reading. Part of this chapter grew out of material that I devised several months before this writing as part of a book I had been contracted to edit. I put in hours of work that

---

* If you are interested in the themes of folk horror, I recommend viewing a remarkable documentary on the genre, *Woodlands Dark and Days Bewitched*. I contributed a historical essay to a book that accompanies the Blu-ray.

exceeded pay. (I would do the same on nearly any project.) Everyone seemed happy. But when it came time to make the second payment in our agreement and enter a new phase of the work, the contracting party demurred. What could I do? Well, not much. But I did experience the benefit of using some of my observations in a meaningful context in this chapter.

This episode further contributed to my observation—made inceptively by Ralph Waldo Emerson in his 1841 essay "Compensation," and personally experienced by me in myriad circumstances—that if you can wait, if you can abide by perspective, the opposing end of a disappointment will eventually result in deliverance. This arrives either in lessons learned, goods procured, relationships entered, achievements attained, or some other manner. Many events *do* seem to have a pendulum of rhythmical balance. This is also among the reasons that Nietzsche more famously observed in *Twilight of the Idols* in 1889, as translated by Kaufmann: "*Out of life's school of war*: What does not destroy me, makes me stronger." The aphorism may be overquoted, often as "what does not kill me." But it is magnetic by dint of truth. As noted, this quid pro quo is not always observable in conventional terms; yet its symmetry often proves traceable over time.

The law of reciprocity means that deceit or absence of plain dealing places you on the negative end of redress. In general, dishonesty places you in service of—and subject to—corrosion versus generativity. The methods of Cosmic Habit Force are the path of *merging with generativity*. You embark on this path through one basic entry point: truthfulness. This means that you side with the forces of growth. You do not serve corrosion. You are protected from what you do not serve.

Let me close with the words of writer and filmmaker Carl Abrahamsson from his *Sacred Intent*, a book of conversations with artist and musician Genesis P-Orridge: "Honesty protects." Etch it on your psyche. It is the code of reciprocity.

HABIT 12

Physical Dynamism

Without physical vitality nothing is possible. If you experience poor health, most of your energy goes to management or recovery. I write this from experience. At the peak of the Covid lockdown in fall 2020, I weighed an unhealthy 216 pounds. As I write these words a year later, I am at 185 pounds and trending downward. As a result, I am more alert, energetic, and capable. Without health as a given, your efforts get diverted.

Health rests on three factors: lifestyle, surrounding environment, and randomness. Lifestyle includes personal practices. It is affected by surrounding environment, which itself includes geography and proximity to healthful conditions. Randomness includes accidents, natural events, and, on the personal scale, innate or genetic predilections. The greater part of all this, for most people, is lifestyle. That factor is largely yours to influence—physically, emotionally, and mentally—and it should be approached with care.

Although many of the "cosmic habits" in this book focus on psyche, work, relations, and conduct, this habit is dedicated expressly to physicality.

I challenge you to something—right now. During the course of reading this book, dedicate 10 consecutive days—a purposefully short and fixed period—to these five habits:

1. **Go clean**. Can you abstain from booze, weed, or drugs for the proposed 10 days? Booze disrupts sleep patterns and productivity. It impedes work. So do many intoxicants. Our nation as a whole is probably imbibing too much of them. This book is not a "dry" program and I am not counseling abstinence (unless you are in a recovery program). But if you cannot abstain from intoxicants for 10 days, you may be facing a problem. A brief period of sobriety may also provide you with important insights about yourself and your energy patterns. If you choose, you can always return to old practices after these 10 days. But this interlude provides a healthful break

and gives you fresh perspective on how you function under both conditions.

2. **100 Pushups a Day**. I realize that this step may require adjustment by the individual—but keep in mind that it is not as difficult as it sounds. And the payoff in mood, self-respect, and physical vibrance are considerable. The only requirement is that you perform 100 pushups daily in a single session broken up into sets however you need or want. If you can do just eight or 10 in a row, that is fine. See how you improve within just a week. This is a cost-free way of getting in shape and benefiting from adjacent mental therapeutics. As of this writing, my partner's grandfather is 93 years old. We joined him on a Zoom call for his birthday, and that day he had done 160 pushups in individual sets of 30. This is a wholly achievable aim.

3. **Regular Meditation**. I practice Transcendental Meditation twice daily. (I am sometimes loose with the times and occasionally miss sessions). To really benefit from a meditation program a steady schedule is necessary. When on track, I sit daily within an hour of waking and again in the late afternoon or early evening. I ask you to try some kind of steady meditative practice during these 10 days. This can

involve "just sitting" for ten minutes twice daily. If you cannot sit still for ten minutes, you cannot do much in life.

4. **Steady With Meds**. As of this writing, I take an SNRI. I am open about that because I do not want such things stigmatized on the path. I reject the nostrum heard in some precincts of the alternative spiritual culture that psychopharmacology is somehow "unspiritual" or cheating. I wear eyeglasses—is that unspiritual? We are physical and extra-physical beings, and life is owed to both realms. The decision to take a drug and how much should always be made with deliberation. Now, when taking a med, consistency is important. If you take meds, dedicate these 10 days to taking them at a fixed time each day in the morning (and again in the afternoon or evening if you dose twice daily). An excellent mental-health counselor named Emily Grossman persuaded me of the importance of steadiness in this respect, and in concurrent habits of sleep and nutrition.

5. **High protein, low carb**. Next to sedentariness or addiction, probably no lifestyle factor is more deleterious to your health than a diet laden with refined carbohydrates and sugars. As is well doc-

umented, such diets contribute to weight gain, pre- and type-two diabetes, hypertension, and other maladies. Whatever you eat—I personally favor a paleo diet—your bulk of calories should come from proteins, with a smaller fraction from complex, unrefined carbs. Sugars, including naturally occurring ones, should be kept at a minimum. Most processed foods are loaded with carbs, sugars, and sodium.

I have selected 10 days not only because it provides enough time to see results but also because it is a sufficiently brief enough period to allow for no reasonable excuses. Ten days is not asking too much. You will detect differences in yourself during this period, and you will see evidence of what a different physical lifestyle can bring. If you already practice healthful habits, the steps in this chapter can augment them. And if you do not, these steps and their revelations might prove personally revolutionary.

As I was writing this chapter, a reader emailed to ask how I maintain my energy levels. "You seem to be everywhere: podcasts, books, forewords in books, giving speeches in various venues," she wrote. "Your overflowing fount of positive energy is inspiring. Also being a parent is quite a time consumer. So, with your positive focus in mind, how does a day go for you? Meditate first thing? Hours reading and researching? Hours writing? Communication time for emails and Facetime?" I replied:

Hi _____, Thanks for your thoughtful note. In all honesty, I would say that the one biggest factor in my time management is passion. I didn't publish my first book until I was past 40 (today I'm 55) so I never take success, readership, or reputation for granted. I feel that it's a privilege every time I'm in front of a microphone or putting my byline on something. Another thing that helps is avoiding or keeping moderate with booze and intoxicants. I like recreational booze or pot, but it simply presents a drag on energy, so I try to eschew it. I avoid refined carbs for the same reason. I exercise, bike almost everywhere (see *The Miracle Month*), and practice Transcendental Meditation twice daily. Having a Definite Chief Aim—and working and praying in that direction—makes a big difference. In fact, it's the decisive difference as an expression of passion. Parenting is a challenge as kids' needs are dynamic and changing, so they will have to write the verdict on whether I've done a good job. Wishing you every good thing,   -Mitch-

*   *   *

Full disclosure: I go through bouts of struggle with smoking, particularly during periods of stress. I enjoy it immensely. The health costs are fearsome in prospect. I find that if I have cigarettes in the home or in my possession the temptation to use them proves overwhelming. It is an addiction.* I have found that the one way to avert a negative health habit is to replace it with a commensurate reward, or the prospect of one. Everything that I describe in this chapter, and all of the benefits I receive, would be abrogated by smoking. I am aided in this realization by the nature of my Definite Chief Aim. If you find that you have a negative health habit that you cannot break, lean on your aim for support. Any kind of unhealthful excess detracts from that aim. If your aim is emotionally driven, if it taps your deepest desires, it should be a help to you in maintenance of sound physical habits since, as we have seen, everything is predicated on some degree of vitality. Your Definite Chief Aim depends on your health. Allow your passion for your aim to support your health.

---

* I return to questions of addiction in Habit 17: *Choose Your Greater Force*.

HABIT 13

Read for Power

Napoleon Hill encouraged "the use of Cosmic Habit Force in developing a system of general self-improvement through study, reading and association with those from whom you may benefit through emulation."

Since you are reading this book, chances are that you are already well-versed in at least one or more of Hill's works. In addition to Hill, I ask you to use this period of exploration to familiarize yourself with several other historical authors who complement and relate to his work. Each was a master of what might be called *the religion of results.* Each will deepen your search and fount of ideas. Some of them played that role for Hill.

The works I recommend reflect America's chief contribution to modern religious life: the principle of spiritual practicality. From early in American history, philosophers, reformers, and mystics have sung the gospel of the functional—of using religious insight as a means to need-fulfillment in the now. They did not necessarily dispense with the salvific qualities of religion; but they saw practicality as a vital and ever-present complement. I believe in the validity of this innovation.

As I have written elsewhere, I see no real line of demarcation between what is commonly regarded as the ineffable and the workaday needs of life; where does one set of concerns begin and another end? Divisions are artificial. We have one existence—some of it visible and sensate, and some of it nonlocal and unseen. But all of it, whole. I think that is a fair statement of the outlook of America's practical religionists, who did more than any other modern voices to unite the needs of materiality and numinosity.

Materiality does not necessarily mean acquisitiveness. In *Walden*, Henry David Thoreau created a manifesto of a life that revolves around cycles of nature and necessity versus busyness and commerce. That Thoreau spent only two years at his lakeside idyll before publishing his 1854 memoir has brought him under literary criticism in recent years from some who view him as more hypester than hermit. But the only real measure of an experimental memoir is the nature of its insight. *Walden* is intended to relate to your life, which is your means for considering its value. Personally, I think artists can reach peaks of understanding without being bound to a program or calendar set by someone else. Truth can arrive in moments, sometimes built on stretches of unheralded prior experience. In that sense, one night of battle can bring greater insight to a sensitive person than a year of trench warfare to another.

Thanks in part to Thoreau, the idea of the individual spiritual search now seems like a birthright. In polls, most Americans—this true in other nations, too—agree that spiritual truth can be found outside of allegiance to any one faith or tradition. "Unaffiliated" is the fastest-growing category of religious identity. In recovery groups, twelve-step programs, and other nontraditional forms of spiritual search (which are explored further in Habit 17), we are encouraged to seek our private conception of a Higher Power or what I call a Greater Force. Even people who affiliate with the traditional faiths are often taught to believe that their own paths to the higher are many—that the gates of prayer and forgiveness are always open; that the seat of the ineffable exists all around us. An element of the Divine, many believe, exists within. Such concepts were foreign, if not heretical, in the hierarchical religiosity of the Old World.

In terms of practicality, this principle of Thoreau's is over-quoted but it is no less enduring for that: "If one advances confidently in the direction of his dreams, and endeavors to live the life which he has imagined, he will meet with a success unexpected in common hours." We expand on Thoreau's insights in Habit 22: *Expect Great Things*.

Ralph Waldo Emerson's essays "Power" and "Wealth," published as separate chapters in his 1860 *The Conduct of Life*, are some of the philosopher's most practical statements on money and enterprise. It is easy and tempting for philosophers to avoid getting plain about such topics. But I truly love that Emerson felt compelled—I think as a matter of debt and respect to his readers—to not only provide metaphysical insights but also a philosophy of *"cash-value"* in life, as William James put it. Will Emerson's essays bring you wealth? I have no idea—but I am certain that their rock-ribbed principles make it impossible to accuse the Yankee Mystic of prevarication or avoidance of what he considered the lived principles of commerce and existence.

In "Power," Emerson names four essential elements to exercising personal power. The first—and that which sustains all the others—is to be "in sympathy with the course of things." Displaying his innate instinct for Taoism and other Eastern philosophies, Emerson believed that an individual could read the *nature of things* and seek to merge with it, like a twig carried downstream. "The mind that is parallel with the laws of nature," he writes, "will be in the current of events, and strong with their strength." This insight forms the core of Cosmic Habit Force.

The second element of power is *health*. Emerson means this on different levels. He is speaking broadly of the vitality of body and spirit; the state of physicality and personal morale that sustains risks, seeks adventure, and completes plans. But he also speaks of routine bodily health, which, as explored in the previous chapter, is a requisite to pursuit of power.

The third element is *concentration*. One of nature's laws is that concentration of energies brings impact. The concentration of a striking blow delivers the greatest force. Recall Bruce Lee's statement from Habit 2: "I fear not the man who has practiced 10,000 kicks once, but I fear the man who has practiced one kick 10,000 times." Too often we deplete our energies by dispersing or spreading thin our aims and efforts. In "Power," an imaginary oracle says: "Enlarge not thy destiny, endeavor not to do more than is given thee in charge." Like light focused into a laser, concentration into a single beam brings the greatest power.

The fourth and final element of power is *drilling*. By this Emerson means repeating a practice over and over until you can perform it with virtuosity. The ballet dancer, gymnast, and martial artist repeat their movements and routines to the point where the moves enter their physical memory and are available to them under all conditions. Likewise, we must drill—or practice or rehearse—to the point where we have mastered our chosen task.

In the essay "Wealth," Emerson declares, chin out, that the individual is "born to be rich." By riches, the philosopher is not employing a coy metaphor. He means cold, hard cash. But he also identifies accumulation of capital as befitting only that person who uses it to productive ends. Emerson writes,

> Every man is a consumer, and ought to be a producer. He fails to make his place good in the world, unless he not only pays his debt, but also adds something to the common wealth. Nor can he do justice to his genius, without making some larger demand on the

world than a bare subsistence. He is by constitution expensive, and needs to be rich.

Only those purchases that expand your power and abilities, Emerson writes, leave you any richer. Indeed, wealth that fails to accompany expansion is wealth thrown away. "Nor is the man enriched," Emerson writes, "in repeating the old experiments of animal sensation." Rather, you are enriched when you increase your ability to earn, to do, and to grow. Wealth, properly understood, is power. That is why these essays are conjoined.

So, how do you earn wealth? Emerson outlines roughly three steps: First, filling some nonnegotiable, subsistence-level need in your own life: this is what drove the primeval farmers, hunter-gatherers, and villagers. Next, applying one's particular talents to nature, and expansively filling the needs of others. If you do not know or understand your talents, you must start there before anything is possible. Your particular talent is a potential source of excellence. And, finally, using your wealth for the purposes of productiveness: paying down debts, making compound investments, and procuring the tools and talents of your trade. Building and expanding are the only sound path to riches. Such things also reflect your code and fiber as a progressing being.

*   *   *

One book that follows Emerson's instincts comes from a writer named for him: Ralph Waldo Trine. Trine's 1897 *In Tune With the Infinite* is an augmented popularization of Thoreau and Emerson's philosophy of Transcendentalism—and also the introduction of New Thought spirituality into the lives of the mass audience that flocked to it. Trine's book cemented the widespread American viewpoint that thoughts are causative, that the mind is a channel of higher laws and cosmic influences, and that a thin tissue, if any, separates mental and spiritual experience.

The power of *In Tune With the Infinite* rests on two counts. The first is that Trine created perhaps not the earliest but, as alluded, the most effective and widely accessible iteration of the New Thought gospel. Trine's popularization remained unrivaled until Norman Vincent Peale published *The Power of Positive Thinking* more than fifty years later in 1952. But Trine's book was something that Peale's was not—and this forms the second basis of its achievement. Although Trine's reference points are chiefly Christian, *In Tune With the Infinite* is one of the first widely popular works of *religious universalism.*

Peale's book was explicitly Christian; the Dutch Reform minister reimagined New Thought in language that was reassuringly familiar to the church-going public. (Although even in this regard Peale included some radically mystical concepts and references.) Trine, by contrast, incorporated principles, if not always language, from broad-spanning religious traditions. In some respects, *In Tune With the Infinite* is as much a popularization of New Thought as it is of Hermetic philosophy. Hermeticism is a late-ancient Greek-Egyptian mystical school that taught that the individual is an extension of a higher mind, or *Nous*, and possesses the same creative potentials. You can see this on display in chapter three, "The Supreme Fact of Human Life," where Trine talks about the nature of the "God-man." In chapter four, "Fullness of Life—Bodily Health and Vigor," Trine remakes the core Hermetic dictum "As above, so below" into "As within, so without; cause, effect." The Hermetic outlook is likewise present when Trine talks about a "divine inflow" into the individual. This also echoes eighteenth-century mystic Emanuel Swedenborg's concept of a "Divine influx."

For all his folksy language, Trine was a radical thinker. And *In Tune With the Infinite*, a book that ultimately sold more than two million copies when the nation itself was far less populous than today, brought everyday Americans ideas that were jarring, fresh, anti-mainstream, and transcendent. That such themes of spiritual possibility sound so familiar to us today is testament to the author's legacy.

Finally, I recommend a hugely influential work that was written not by an American but a British seeker: *As a Man Thinketh* by James Allen. In terms of influence, Allen probably surpassed even Trine, as his 1903 meditation remains widely read today while his American counterpart's is not. Allen wrote compellingly that outer experience reflects inner life, and that refinement within lawfully pictures without.

Allen's book is marked by memorable, aphoristic lessons, which have withstood the passage of time. *As a Man Thinketh* defines achievement in deeply personal terms: "You will become as small as your controlling desire; as great as your dominant aspiration."

Toward the end of *As a Man Thinketh*, Allen, a man of working-class roots, writes in a manner that amounts to autobiography:

Here is a youth hard pressed by poverty and labor; confined long hours in an unhealthy workshop; unschooled, and lacking all the arts of refinement. But he dreams of better things: he thinks of intelligence, of refinement, of grace and beauty. He conceives of, mentally builds up, an ideal condition of life; vision of a wider liberty and a larger scope takes possession of him; unrest urges him to action, and he utilizes all his spare time and means, small though they are, to the development of his latent powers and resources. Very soon so altered has his mind become that the workshop can no longer hold him.

As a personal rule, Allen always used his life experiences as the backbone of his teaching. "He never wrote *theories*," his wife Lily noted in 1913, "or for the sake of writing; but he wrote when he had a message, and it became a message *only when he had lived it out in his own life*, and knew that it was good."

None of these works, powerful as each is, is complete in itself. That fact should stir you to further questions. I personally believe that New Thought, a philosophy I love, has never fully developed a theology of suffering or adequately captured the complexity of disease and illness as something more than thought forms. On a related note, I believe in, and follow, the ideas set down by Emerson; yet I am also mindful that he came from an affluent New England family and his observations about self-reliance, independent living, and radical individualism would have differed if written by a working person. (He disputed this point but I am not so sure.) Thoreau, finally, is a hero to me but my territory for testing his truths has been urban rather than rural, a difference to which he may not have ultimately objected.

My point here is that I want you to experience these works on your own terms; test their usefulness through application; and bring your own questions out of them. "Spirituality" is not a closed-circuit but a field of discovery where we wish to understand our connections to greater laws and forces. Let this short reading list serve as a rung to your own discovery. May you surpass that rung.

HABIT 14

Attitude of Earning

In late 2020, I was touched by the candor of a therapist on Twitter who tweeted: "As a therapist I can say confidently, that while therapy is helpful, what most people really need is money." Given that the number of retweets at the time exceeded 100,000, her honesty clearly resonated. There were also vocal critics. I personally considered her statement an important acknowledgment.

Napoleon Hill would have concurred that sometimes—and probably often—people simply need more money. Writing with probity, mind-power mystic Joseph Murphy observed in *The Power of Your Subconscious*

Mind in 1963, "I believe most people are inadequately compensated." I want to offer you four steps on how to earn more. I have used them in my life. They are simple. But look twice at them. It is only when you apply or live with a seemingly simple idea that its greater dimensions appear. That is why cynics rarely get at the truth of things. They see simplicity as naïveté. Simplicity is the language of truth.

1. **You must sincerely and powerfully desire to earn more**. Doesn't everyone? Well, not exactly. This does not mean an unspecified wish to "get rich." Or a "sure, why not?" attitude. It means a burning and specific desire to increase your earning ability. And be specific: how much do you want to earn and how? Don't vacillate. Name a reasonable amount. If you have not already, you must read Napoleon Hill's *Think and Grow Rich*. If you have already read it, read it again. I reread it once a year. I often advise readers to do its exercises *as though their lives depend on it*. If you do, things will change for the better.

2. **One victory naturally leads to another**. What you do on a micro scale can be repeated on a macro scale. Again, the Hermetic dictum: "as above, so below." One act of earning extra money teaches you your capability and generally leads to further increase.

Do not overshoot and get disappointed. Be focused, clear, and active. When you succeed, you will have discovered a steppingstone.

3. **Cultivate skill and excellence**. This principle encompasses many things. You must not only do a job well and expeditiously, but you must keep up with the technology of your field. This is not always easy for me. I am tech-shy. But I impel myself to stay current. When I fall behind, I strive to compensate for it. Another thing that cultivates excellence is sobriety, as alluded in Habit 12. Like many people, I enjoy booze and other intoxicants. But, as noted, they can disrupt sleep patterns, foster lethargy, and contribute to negative or obsessive thoughts. Even if temporarily, stop drinking or using recreational drugs when you wish to earn more. Here is a different ingredient to excellence, as well as reputation: pay your debts quickly, especially to contractors and freelancers. Such an act fosters comity and loyalty. Those people depend on your timely payment as another does on his or her paycheck. Pay them quickly and they become dedicated allies.

4. **Expeditiousness**. When offered opportunities to earn, *act decisively*. Never dither. I was once offered a large book contract for which I felt unprepared. I

quickly caught myself and said yes. It was one of the best decisions of my life. Growing up, my mother told me never to refuse business. That was sound advice. I am shocked when I see storeowners, managers, or contractors turn away business. Actually turn away people who want to pay them for a service and who need their service. I saw this occur even during the Covid recession. In Brooklyn, New York, where I live, I witnessed computer and bicycle stores turn away customers—or shun them by requiring weeks-long waits—rather than expand, hire new people (a greatly productive thing to do for your community, especially during a recession), and embrace new business. To me, refusing work is one of the most deleterious of practices. There is always an excuse to say no. Rarely a good one. Do not be that person.

In a different vein, some of us find it difficult to claim and accept legitimately earned rewards. We may feel that a certain honor, award, promotion, or other form of credit or recognition does not fully belong to us. A person may feel stymied by the perception that a successful project resulted from a group effort—which is a legitimate realization, as everything depends on multiple efforts; or that claiming an achievement seems conceited or inflated. But the ability to attain your goals rests in part on your willingness to recognize and claim just victory.

Some people have the opposite problem. They rush to claim ownership over something to which they were only tangentially connected, or they exaggerate their role or title. That is an ethical lapse; it means obfuscating accomplishments that belong to others. But the habit of *accepting legitimate credit* is a worthy practice for productive and principled people; people who truly contribute to their surroundings and act on the kinds of ideas found in this book—but who also have difficulty acknowledging and announcing their achievements. This is a more general problem than it may first appear.

The cultivation of purpose and excellence is so important that I want to revisit the question from a different angle. In 1854, the pioneering scientist and germ theorist Louis Pasteur said in a lecture: "In the fields of observation chance favors only the prepared mind." This statement has been popularly—and, I think, accurately—shortened into: "Chance favors the prepared mind." If you want to foster greater earning opportunities in your life, make it your motto.

Chance opportunities are useful only to those who are ready for them—the greater your preparation the more fully you will be able to take advantage of them when they arrive. Preparation requires training, studying, reliability, keeping your word, and showing up ready to perform whatever task you face. It heightens all of the other random factors around you; it ensures that you are in the right mental state to notice, receive, and profit from opportunities. That is why I do not believe in opportunities just coming "out of the blue." Opportunities occur in context.

Motivational pioneer Dale Carnegie (1888–1955) began his career in the early twentieth century as a teacher of public speaking. A former actor, Carnegie grasped as early as 1912, when he began teaching his first classes, that public speaking was becoming a vital part of business. When preparing a talk or pitch, Carnegie advised that you should amass so much material that you discard 90 percent of it when actually speaking. The very fact of your preparation gives you the confidence and power to present without notes, and to deliver a more relaxed, enthusiastic, and freestyle performance.

Carnegie's formula is a recipe for good outcomes and earning in every area of life. Once you are justifiably confident and expert in a task or project, you can watch, listen, intuit, and become aware of important cues. Ardent preparation makes you persuasive. Your actions grow natural and effortless. You can pivot. You convey confidence. You may even gain a childlike exuberance. When opportunities appear, such as a job opening, an audition, a call to present on the fly at a conference, or even being seated next to your boss or a senior manager on an air flight, the prepared person will be able to seize the moment.

Not only does fortune favor the prepared mind, so does earning.

HABIT 15

Cultivate Inner Power

Napoleon Hill often wrote about the nature of Infinite Intelligence which flows through each individual. Hill's definition of Infinite Intelligence agreed with what Ralph Waldo Emerson wrote in his essay "History" in 1841: "There is one mind common to all individual men. Every man is an inlet to the same and to all of the same."

Hill wrote that a Master Mind alliance, in which two or more participants regularly gather to encourage one another's aims, taps into the power of Infinite Intelligence. A Master Mind group is Infinite Intelligence localized to a small, harmonious group of people.* I was interested to later discover that Hill referred to Cosmic Habit Force in another unpublished talk as "Infinite Intelligence in operation." He believed in a kind of over-mind—a nonlocalized intellect to which we are all attached, as oceans feed channels. He also encouraged using visualizations, prayer, and affirmations as ways of tapping the insights and causative powers of Infinite Intelligence through the medium of your subconscious. The subconscious, Hill taught, translates thoughts, plans, and ideas to Infinite Intelligence for actualization, the power of which returns to you in the form of flashes of insight, leads, and intuitions. Infinite Intelligence, in Hill's view, uses the individual as its medium of creation.

"If you conceive a thing and believe it and make a definite picture of it in your own mind," Hill said in a lecture to his Success Unlimited class, "the law of Cosmic Habit Force takes over that picture and guides you to the physical equivalent of that thing, whatever it may be . . . And you'll be surprised at how many things will come to you that you wanted before, that you worked hard for and didn't get when you learn how to fasten upon your mind a definite outline of the things that represent to you success in this life."

---

* For further exploration, see my book *The Power of the Master Mind*.

Hill's point of view was more or less in alignment with that of New Thought pioneer Geneviève Behrend (1881–1960). The author and seeker—herself a close student of mind theorist Thomas Troward (1847–1916)—provided a clarifying portrait of her metaphysical principles in her 1921 volume *Your Invisible Power*. They sound much like Hill's own and warrant parallel exploration:

We now fly through the air, not because anyone has been able to change the laws of Nature, but because the inventor of the flying machine learned how to apply Nature's laws and, by making orderly use of them, produced the desired result. So far as the natural forces are concerned, nothing has changed since the beginning. There were no airplanes in "the Year One," because those of that generation could not conceive the idea as a practical, working possibility. "It has not yet been done," was the argument, "and it cannot be done." Yet the laws and materials for practical flying machines existed then as now.

Troward tells us that the great lesson he learned from the airplane and wireless telegraphy is the triumph of principle over precedent, the working out of an idea to its logical conclusion in spite of accumulated contrary testimony of all past experience.

Behrend's perspective, like Hill's, does not endorse the idea that your visualizing powers will manifest properties from the ether. (I prefer the term *select* to manifest, a choice I expand on in *The Miracle Club*.) Rather, the powers of causative thought can bring about the extraordinary by working through *established channels* of creation. We do not bend natural laws, in Hill's view—we discover multitudinous possibilities within them. Likewise, Behrend puts it this way, with her emphasis in the original: "*In visualizing, or making a mental picture, you are not endeavoring to change the laws of Nature. You are fulfilling them.*"

Compare that to Hill's perspective from an undated audio presentation about Cosmic Habit Force:

The same force which maintains the precise balance between all the actions and reactions of matter and the time and space relationships of the elements of Creation also builds man's thought habits with varying degrees of permanency. Negative thought habits of any kind attract to their Creator physical manifestations corresponding to their nature as perfectly and as inevitably as nature germinates the acorn and develops it into an oak tree. Through the operation of the very same law, positive thoughts reach out into the vast ocean of potential power surrounding us and attract the physical counterparts of their nature.

You create patterns of thought by repeating certain ideas or behavior and the law of Cosmic Habit Force takes over those patterns and makes them more or less permanent unless or until you consciously rearrange them. The method employed by Cosmic Habit Force in converting a positive emotion or desire created in the mind of man into its physical equivalent is this: It intensifies that emotion or desire until it induces the state of mind known as faith, in which it is receptive to inflowing Infinite Intelligence whence are derived perfect plans to be followed by the individual for the attainment of his desired objective. Natural means are used to carry out such plans.

Often a person is awed by what appear to be coincidental combinations of favorable circumstances as he carries out his plans, but these strange and unexplained things happen in a perfectly natural way. Cosmic Habit Force has the capacity to impart a peculiar quality to one's thought habits which gives them the power to surmount all difficulties, remove all obstacles, overcome all resistances. Just what this power is, is a secret as profound as the secret which causes a seed of wheat to germinate, grow, and reproduce itself.

Hence, both systems agree that although the individual must function within the physical sphere in which he finds himself—subject to its limits and natural laws—he is also an extension of Infinite Intelligence and functions as a channel of creative ability whose method is thought.

Whether you are new to these ideas or whether you are a veteran reader who, like me, needs a refresher in mind power, let me propose an exercise: Reread the statements above from Behrend and Hill. When you are finished, select and dedicate one hour—just one hour—during which you will assume that the writers' *every premise about thought and creation is correct*. Act as though you possess ultimate creative responsibility for your life. Entertain no doubts. This is your private experiment. Tell no one what you are doing. Behrend provides wise counsel on how speech dissipates the impact of thought: "One tells one's troubles to weaken them, to get them off one's mind, and when a thought is given out, its power is dissipated."

If your *one hour* leaves you satisfied, select another period in which to expand your experiment to two hours. Then expand two to four, four to eight, and, finally, eight to sixteen, which is, roughly, the length of a waking day. Once you reach the waking-day stage of your experiment, go to sleep visualizing a desired outcome. That final step amounts to a 24-hour commitment. See what occurs. Will you try? It requires only one hour to start.

If you experience doubts or setbacks, do not worry. There is no need to start over. Life is filled with switchbacks. It is unrealistic and unnecessary to attempt to avoid them. You are not seeking an impossibly high standard of inner performance. You are simply exploring your dimensions as an ethical and creative being—and probing "your invisible power" as a self-devised, or at least co-created, being.

I now want to take things a step further and offer you an exercise in creative visualization. The type of visualization I often use is prescribed by twentieth century mystic Neville Goddard (1905–1972): play in your mind a small scene or sensation that implies the fulfillment of your aim. It can be anything, as long as it is vivid, tactile, and emotive. *Feel yourself* in any small drama or role, no matter how brief, that would naturally accompany the arrival of your wish, such as someone shaking your hand and congratulating you. You are not watching the image as if it is on a screen—rather, you are feeling and imagining yourself *within* the scenario.

The best times to enter this state, I have found, are when you are drifting to sleep at night—a period of natural relaxation called hypnagogia—or other periods when you may feel a sense of bodily relaxation, such as following meditation. *But do not be controlled by form.* When you arrive at a moment where an inner scene or a sense of quietude, or both, reach you: act on it.

Recent to this writing, I was just standing in my kitchen in Brooklyn, New York, and felt a sense of the kind of scene that implied the fulfillment I wished for. I was awake before anyone else in my household, so I went into a meditative state and *internally* acted out the scene. Were it any other time of day I would have done the same, if at all possible. You must act when the mood strikes. Never mind whether you have the "ideal" hour of day or privacy. These are precious moments. Use them.

Further pursuing the visualization method, I want to share an exercise that reached me in the form of an email from a reader. It was accompanied by a powerful and personal backstory which I omit for reasons of privacy, sticking only with the technique that was offered:

If you could do anything in your life from where you are, if money was no problem, what would you want to do? Your big goal, the thing that would fill you up. What job would you love to do if family, education, and money didn't come into it? Write down your goals for this year with as much detail as you can imagine. Get quiet and visualize them like they are already real. Feel what it would be like if they had already happened. See yourself doing those things, being happy and living it. Your friends congratulating you and being amazed at what you've achieved. What are they saying to you? They're shocked and high fiving you!

Do the imagining every night for about 15 days before you go to sleep and really put feeling and emotions into the visions. Feel the excitement. This really works, it will put things into motion but you have to believe in it. Trust in this and give it a try.

I suggest writing out this quoted passage by hand, adding the words "I trust" at the bottom, dating it, and signing it. I did this. Because I never suggest anything that I do not do myself.

One final note: to attain her goal of becoming a personal student of retired judge and mind theorist Thomas Troward, Geneviève Behrend did not only think, feel, and visualize—she acted: with persistence, some degree of audacity, and aplomb. She kept after Troward—doggedly but intelligently—even after the metaphysical writer first ignored and then refused her entreaties. She impressed her hoped-for teacher not only by her resiliency but also by *her rigor of preparation*. Never neglect that.

This touches on how I came to collaborate with Josh T. Romero, a gifted graphic artist, musician, and website designer. In spring of 2020, Josh sought to work with me. He made a video pitching himself—a step that I really appreciated. He followed up by creating several pieces of promotional art for events I was doing. They were brilliant—relevant, margin-pushing, and fresh. Within about five months, I opted to formalize our relationship and today we collaborate on a wide range of projects. Josh began it all, he told me, by holding an ideal in his mind—and he also acted.

"A great idea is valueless," Behrend wrote, "unless accompanied by physical action."

HABIT 16

Genius and Sex Transmutation

Toward the end of his life, the pioneering psychical researcher Frederic Myers (1843–1901) pondered the nature and origins of genius. The British scientist came to believe that genius, or remarkable inspiration and application of ideas, possessed an origin or at least an element outside of the everyday mind. Myers called it the *supraliminal mind*.

In his posthumously published 1903 treatise *Human Personality and Its Survival of Bodily Death*, the researcher wrote:

Genius—if that vaguely used word is to receive any-thing like a psychological definition—should rather be regarded as a power of utilising a wider range than other men can utilise of faculties in some degree innate in all;—a power of appropriating the results of subliminal mentation to subserve the supralim-inal stream of thought;—so that an "inspiration of Genius" will be in truth a *subliminal uprush*, an emergence into the current of ideas which the man is consciously manipulating of other ideas which he has not consciously originated, but which have shaped themselves beyond his will, in profounder regions of his being. I shall urge that there is here no real departure from normality; no abnormality, at least in the sense of degeneration; but rather a fulfilment of the true norm of man, with suggestions, it may be, of something *supernormal*;—of something which transcends existing normality as an advanced stage of evolutionary progress transcends an earlier stage.

In short, Myers saw genius as an interplay between the subliminal or subconscious mind—a concept that his work also helped define and establish—and a supra-liminal mind, or what Napoleon Hill called Infinite Intelligence. In Myers' view, this interplay resulted in genius, a perspective that is in harmony with Hill's outlook. Hill added a powerful adjunct to this schema:

genius, or inspired thought, can be accessed through the method of *sex transmutation.*

Hill saw sex transmutation—the process of channeling sexual desire into inspiration—as a critical facet of Cosmic Habit Force. Hill spoke of using "the application of the law of Cosmic Habit Force in developing a system for transmuting sex emotion by directing it through creative habits connected with your major purpose in life." He continued in 1952,

I can remember the time when even the very word "sex" couldn't be mentioned in mixed company. As a matter of fact, that great emotion is the creative device of nature, through which she perpetuates all living species. And I have never found a great outstanding person yet, in the pulpit, in law, in medicine, in authorship, in public speaking, in art nor in any other calling that was not a highly sexed person who had learned how to transmute that great emotion into the constructive things represented with that person's major objective in life. In the very nature of the subject, I can't go into finer details in an audience like this, but certainly it is up to you to learn the possibilities of making use of the law of Cosmic Habit Force in transmuting that great creative emotion of nature into the things that you wish to accomplish in this life.

As Hill alluded, the of topic sex transmutation is one of his most subtle and powerful teachings. It remains controversial. Even some contemporary interpreters sidestep the topic by redubbing it "enthusiasm" when reviewing Hill's methods. But Hill was plain on the matter, writing about it first in *Think and Grow Rich* in 1937 and later in *Think Your Way to Wealth* in 1948:

> The emotion of sex is nature's own source of inspiration through which she gives both men and women the impelling desire to create, build, lead, and direct. Every great artist, every great musician, and every great dramatist gives expression to the emotion of sex transmuted into human endeavor.

In Hill's outlook, the urge toward sexuality is the creative impulse of life expressing itself through the individual, just as Infinite Intelligence expresses itself through the atmosphere of the Master Mind group. But Hill also taught—and this is the inner key to sex transmutation and other ancient and modern traditions that employ the sexual urge—that sexuality goes far beyond matters of intimacy and reproduction; sexuality expresses itself in every facet of human creativity. Through this creative impulse we are driven to function as generative beings in all ways—commercially and artistically, as well as in health, trade, communication, travel, culture, and finance. Whenever you strive to actualize your visions in the world you are, he said, operating from the vital, life-building impulse that we term sexuality.

Once you cultivate this awareness you can *transmute* the sexual urge into improved performance, focus, and insight in matters of wealth, art, or anything on which you elect to focus. The method is simplicity itself: *When you experience the sexual urge, you redirect your thoughts and energies along the lines of a cherished project or piece of work. Through the mental act of redirecting yourself from physical expression to creative expression you harness and place the sexual urge at the back of your efforts.* Doing so, Hill taught, adds vigor, creativity, and intellectual prowess to your work.

It is important to note that Hill did not call for celibacy or the general sublimation of sexuality in its physical form. In fact, he underscored the importance of sex not only as a physical release but also for therapeutic and stress-reducing purposes, as well as a core part of intimacy. Rather, his point is that you are capable, at times of your choosing, to harness this innate life force to elevate your energies and abilities in a manner far beyond what you may consider possible. Again, this is a mental act performed privately and at moments of your selection: when you experience the sexual urge, rather than immediately satisfying it physically, you instead redirect your thoughts toward a specific goal or task. This places heightened insight, perspicacity, enthusiasm, and vigor behind your efforts.

Understanding sexuality as a supraliminal force squares with Frederic Myers' outlook on the nature of genius. Indeed, Hill argued that figures who are commonly regarded as geniuses, icons, or impresarios can rise to that level of excellence *because sexual energy is at the back of their efforts*. This energy is the force of creation seeking expression through us in myriad ways.

Now, for the plural term geniuses, Hill used the arcane plural *genii*. This is significant. Genii dates to Roman-Latin usage. It means not only intellectual prowess but also suggests the Ancient Roman meaning—updated by Myers—that genius itself is a gift bestowed by higher spirits or daemons. The same term appears as *jinn* or genie in Arab folklore and culture, again referencing a spirit capable of possessing the individual or bestowing supernatural power. This further suggests the connection that Hill saw between numinous forces of life and the individual's capacity for accomplishment.

Let me offer a somewhat idiosyncratic but entirely real encounter with sex transmutation, one that is both recent to this writing and, by its quotidian nature, may prove broadly relevant.

I maintain a small audio and video studio in my apartment, which I use for digital lectures and events. The studio is outfitted with a large set of blackout curtains so that I can control the lighting. One evening, one of my kids accidentally pulled down the curtain rods from the wall. I refastened them—with mixed results. I live in a Victorian-era home in Brooklyn and we do our best to take care of the walls, moldings, sconces, and other period details. But when remounting the curtains, I made a bit of a mess of things. The plaster is flakey, and it took me several tries to get it right. My effort was not right enough. One night—don't ask me how—one of the kids pulled down the curtains yet again. It was too late to work on the job, so I put it off to the morning. But—and this is just one of those odd personal peccadillos that I am sure you have felt in certain areas of your own life—I was anxious and self-obsessed over the matter. For various reasons, a lot of emotion got mixed in with this: Was I properly caring for my home? Was I supervising my kids? Did I know how to adequately repair things? Would I cause harm to the features of the historic house? Every one of these things had a rational answer but I was functioning from my emotions; rationality seemed distant.

As I lay awake that night, I vowed to try an experiment. Although I am no whiz at home repair, I vowed to use sex transmutation in the service of doing a killer job on reinstalling those curtains. I would not only make it right but I would repair the previous damage and secure them in a way that both honored the delicateness of the walls and created a fastening that not even King Kong could dislodge. On a rainy morning, I reentered the studio, sized up the situation, and went out to purchase spackle, anchors, and other fix-it supplies. And I simply killed it. On every count. I preserved the historical details, repaired the old damage, and securely fastened the brackets. Here are the pictures.

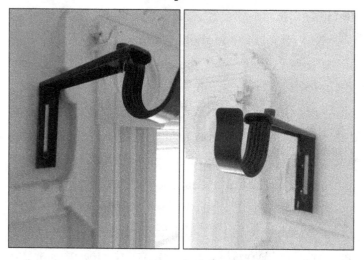

Perhaps Michelangelo has nothing to worry about; but as an urban dweller who is caring for a private home for the first time, I stepped up. I experienced the power and energy of sex transmutation at the back of my efforts. I purposefully selected a simple—even an easily grinned at—example to make a point about applicability. Let it serve as encouragement for your own experiments of whatever nature.

Sex transmutation is a wonderful method artistically, professionally, domestically, and financially. But there are, of course, periods when cultivation of inner power, persistence, and methods like sex transmutation fall short. During periods of grief, anxiety, despair, or when buffeted by the waves of addiction, we may find that we need a *Greater Force* on which to rely. I heartily endorse searching for and working with such a power, which informs our next cosmic habit.

HABIT 17

Choose Your Greater Force

Napoleon Hill often wrote about the existence of Infinite Intelligence, as explored in Habit 15: *Cultivate Inner Power*. Infinite Intelligence was Hill's personal conception of and term for a Higher Power. The concept of a Higher Power—an extra-physical force or source of creation selected through the individual's private understanding, requiring neither sectarian attachment nor approval—was popularized by a determined and ingenious group of seekers contemporaneous to Hill. Their seminal text appeared two years after Hill published *Think and Grow Rich* in 1937: *Alcoholics Anonymous* written by Bill Wilson (1885–1971) and his collaborators, including his wife and intellectual part-ner Lois Wilson (1891–1988) and his companion in the search for recovery, Dr. Bob Smith (1879–1950).

Although initially designed for alcoholism, the AA approach gave birth to the modern recovery movement. Its twelve-step model was later used to treat problems encompassing drug addiction, compulsive gambling, weight control, excessive spending, and chronic anger. AA altered the language of American life, giving rise to expressions such as "easy does it," "one day at a time," "first things first," and "let go and let God." As noted, its literature also popularized an ecumenical term for God or a Creator: "Higher Power." This phrase appeared in the group's key principle that the alcoholic's "defense must come from a Higher Power," as Bill Wilson wrote in 1939. But Wilson and Smith insisted that twelve-steppers must form *their own* conception of God "*as we understood Him*," as the third step went. "Higher Power" captured the radical ecumenism they were after.*

Indeed, the group's emphasis on a nondenom-inational Higher Power was even more radical and

---

* The term Higher Power probably entered AA's lexicon through Ralph Waldo Trine's 1897 New Thought bestseller, *In Tune With the Infinite*, a favorite book of Bob Smith's. Trine repeatedly used the term, with partic-ular reference to alcohol: "In the degree that we come into the realization of the higher powers of the mind and spirit . . . there also falls away the desire for the heavier, grosser, less valuable kinds of food and drink, such as the flesh of animals, alcoholic drinks . . ." I go further into the history of AA in my *One Simple Idea: How Positive Thinking Reshaped Modern Life*.

unorthodox in its early days. AA received major national exposure and validation from an extensive and sympathetic article by journalist Jack Alexander in the March 1, 1941, edition of *The Saturday Evening Post*. Alexander wrote about what a newcomer could expect from the group:

> If he applies to Alcoholics Anonymous, he is first brought around to admit that alcohol has him whipped and that his life has become unmanageable. Having achieved this state of intellectual humility he is given a dose of religion in the broadest sense. He is asked to believe in a Power that is greater than himself, or at least to keep an open mind on that subject while he goes on with the rest of the program. Any concept of the Higher Power is acceptable. A skeptic or agnostic may choose to think of his Inner Self, the miracle of growth, a tree, man's wonderment at the physical universe, the structure of the atom, or mere mathematical infinity. Whatever form is visualized, the neophyte is taught that he must rely upon it and, in his own way, to pray to the Power for strength.

This is the type of heterodox and open-sourced spirituality that I endorse in this cosmic habit. Now, I believe in the general nature of the AA approach; I believe that there are moments when life's burdens overwhelm us and require petitioning some energy of a greater nature. Yet some seekers are uncomfortable with even the nonsectarian term Higher Power as it still rests within the assumptions of the hierarchical or Abrahamic religious model. This is why I personally favor the term *Greater Force*.

A Greater Force can be anything representative of the extra-physical nature of life. It can be an ancient deity with which you feel resonance. It can be what the Hermetic Greeks called *Nous* or a higher mind; what Ralph Waldo Emerson called the Over-Soul; what Napoleon Hill called Infinite Intelligence; or what scientist-mystic Emanuel Swedenborg called the Divine Influx. Your Greater Force can even be the cycle of Cosmic Habit Force itself—the innate and eternal order that maintains all of life, like the concept of Tao in ancient Chinese philosophy.

I am not an atheist, but I like Jack Alexander's ardent secularization of the concept of a Greater Force: "A skeptic or agnostic may choose to think of his Inner Self, the miracle of growth, a tree, man's wonderment at the physical universe, the structure of the atom, or mere mathematical infinity." (I am unsettled on the question, but in Alexander's framing, a Definite Chief Aim could also serve as that Greater Force.) If, for example, a person thinks in materialistic terms, it may be possible to read the work of a philosopher like Ayn Rand who elevates human will to the position of the highest expression of life. Rand's expression of the seminal importance of *nowness* is not dissimilar to principles found in Zen. Critics see in a Rand a figure excessively committed to acquisitiveness or a ruthless (and sometimes hypocritical) form of economic Social Darwinism; but, in actuality, Rand's core outlook is one of human expressiveness, albeit without conventional conceptions of service, community, or altruism, which she perceived, at least as traditionally expressed, as ethically muddled, ill-defined, and diversionary. For some readers, that is a dealbreaker. Hence, Rand's critics see her as maleficent (or a *Mean Girl* as a recent critical study is titled). Although I find Rand's tone too absolutist and bellicose (which she, in turn, would attribute to my own ethical confusion) it would be an error to conclude that the author was unmoved by human suffering. She considered *application of the will* the only lasting solution to suffering. Claims of altruism, in her view, are often disguised means of dictatorial behavior or the wish to control another. If you like these ideas but resonate with a more occult aesthetic, you can also investigate the work of artist, provocateur, and Church of Satan founder Anton LaVey, who prescribed application of the will and his own style of what I call "Positive Thinking Weaponized."

In any case, no perspective on belief is required, in my estimation, to conceive of, experiment with, and draw upon the greater forces of life. If this book succeeds, it is a manual in doing so. We revisit this theme in our final chapter.

HABIT 18

You Are Only as Good as Your Word

Many years ago, I published a book by a deeply intelligent and serious author who was part of a circle of neo-pagan and nature-based occult seekers in England. They held themselves to high standards. Their first and chief principle: keep your word.

It is a tough truth of life: *If you cannot keep your word, you can do nothing.*

No single practice does more to strip away fantasies of "enlightenment," mawkish sharing of experiences, forced intimacies, inflated sense of advancement, or other maladies of our alternative spiritual scene than the application of this one simple standard—provided it is done with integrity and self-observation.

Striving to keep your word means sometimes failing. But to acknowledge that failure—and to feel it—is a help in itself. You must never use that acknowledgment as evasion, however, a dodge or trick we too quickly learn. True acknowledgment involves suffering.

I want to share a story from Fritz Peters' 1964 memoir *Boyhood with Gurdjieff*, a haunting and powerful record. In Peters' book, the author recounts the commitment exacted from him by the Greek-Armenian spiritual teacher G.I. Gurdjieff (1866–1949) when he was eleven years old. The adolescent met Gurdjieff in June 1924 when he was sent to spend the summer at the teacher's school, the Prieuré, a communal estate in Fontainebleau-Avon outside of Paris. Speaking to Fritz on a stone patio one day, Gurdjieff banged the table with his fist and asked, "Can you promise to do something for me?"

The boy gave a firm, "Yes."

The teacher gestured to the estate's vast expanse of lawns. "You see this grass?" he asked.

"Yes," Fritz said again.

"I give you work. You must cut this grass, with machine, every week."

Fritz agreed—but that wasn't enough. Gurdjieff "struck the table with his fist for the second time. 'You must promise on your God.' His voice was deadly serious. 'You must promise that you will do this thing no matter what happens.'"

Fritz replied, "I promise."

Again, not enough. "Not just promise," Gurdjieff said. "Must promise you will do no matter what happens, no matter who try stop you. Many things can happen in life."

Fritz vowed again.

Many things can happen in life. Very soon, in the lives of Fritz and his teacher, something seismic and upending did occur. Gurdjieff suffered a severe car accident and for several weeks laid in a near-coma recovering at the Prieuré. Fritz, feeling that the whole thing seemed almost foreordained, honored his commitment to keep mowing the lawns. But he met with stern resistance. Several adults at the school insisted to him that the noise would disturb Gurdjieff's convalescence and could even result in the master's death. Fritz recalled how unsparingly the promise had been exacted and how fully it had been given. He refused to relent. He kept mowing—and no one physically stopped him. One day while Fritz was cutting the lawns, he spied the recovering master smile at him from his bedroom window.

I think I have captured this episode accurately, at least insofar as the author related it. This is not easy to do. The spiritual teacher Gurdjieff cannot be easily summarized in his lessons or in any of the episodes surrounding his life. People often attempt to compare Gurdjieff's ideas or methods to other things or to restate them: "Oh, it's like . . ." A colleague of mine once said, "It's not *like* anything."

I note this to come around to a related point. The greatest benefit I personally received from the Gurdjieff work was the stripping away of fantasies.

We in the modern West are suffused with contra-dictions. In one of those contradictions, we are taught, over and over—corporately, educationally, therapeu-tically, spiritually—how great we are. People are filled with puffed up views of themselves. (They are also filled with the opposite—we receive confounding messages.) We are often told that we are "special" so we can be sold things. New Age culture, which does many good things, also encourages this "I'm special" attitude. But take one person and give him or her an unfamiliar task at an inconvenient hour and you will see how powerful or special we are. Not very.

Keeping your word is a way of measuring yourself. It reveals your relationships and how others experience you. Alcoholics Anonymous co-founder Bill Wilson, who we encountered in the previous chapter, made the important observation that progress is best measured by others—we have an ego-filter but others tend to see us first and most clearly. How others see and experience you rests heavily on the extent to which you keep your word.

Habit 18 is simple. Simple in the sense of basic. But it goes to the heart of who you are.

Keeping your word, or not lying as seen in Habit 10, or eschewing some familiar comfort, if done with true intention, are sources of power because *they strip away theatrics and delusion*; and, if successful, such measures leave standing your more authentic self. Others observe and respond to that. That is the true definition of being oneself. Let it start with keeping your word.

There is an adjunct to this point. Earlier I quoted Nietzsche: "Formula for our happiness: a Yes, a No, a straight line, a goal." When you agree to do a favor for someone, or you pledge your help with something, do it fully. Yes means yes—not *yes-minus* or *yes-but* or *maybe* (which is really just a slow-motion no). Withholding full assistance is rarely indicative of critical judgment or discretion; most often it is parsimoniousness or passive-aggression. And it is experienced as such. A key insight into whether someone will prove a reliable partner, friend, business associate, or interlocuter is the degree to which he or she fully delivers on what is pledged. Or, by contrast, has the forthrightness to simply say *no*.

In any case: never provide someone with a half-glass of water. When you say yes, go all the way.

Keeping your word also means striving to *do for self*. Imagine the changes that could ripple through your life, your self-image, and your relationships if you internalized this principle: *Overly depending on others erodes your sense of self-respect as it also erodes your basic abilities and acumen.*

Recent to this writing, I caught myself slipping into a minor pattern of dependency in matters of cooking, food prep, and meal planning. I saw the effects accumulating and vowed to reverse course. Doing so strengthened my relationships and household. It rippled through several areas of my life.

Relationships, careers, and households often experience turning points over seemingly small things. Anything that becomes a repository, symbol, or fulcrum for *emotion* dramatically affects your surrounding environment. This can be as small as either making or leaving a bed unmade habitually.

I believe that a small commitment, made passionately and lived by (even if fitfully) can change your world. Even the world. Imagine if just 10 percent of the public, or even 1 percent, took this vow—and meant it:

I will first make every effort to meet my own needs before requesting assistance from another; I will enlist another's help only when matters of personal wellbeing or safety are involved or I have made every reasonable effort on my own.

We harbor enormous resentment of others—*and shame of self*—over matters of superfluous dependency. For your part, break that cycle.

HABIT 19

Discover Your Polarity

I experienced a revolutionary moment in life while I was in Denver in spring 2018 to deliver a series of talks. In my hotel room one day, I read this passage from *Think and Grow Rich*:

> O. Henry discovered the genius which slept within his brain, after he had met with great misfortune, and was confined to a prison cell in Columbus, Ohio. Being FORCED, through misfortune, to become acquainted with his "other self," and to use his IMAGINATION, he discovered himself to be a great author instead of a miserable criminal and outcast.

Strange and varied are the ways of life, and stranger still are the ways of Infinite Intelligence, through which men are sometimes forced to undergo all sorts of punishments before discovering their own brains, and their own capacity to create useful ideas through imagination.

I knew something as a fact at that moment—in the way you experience a fact of self when discovering that another person with whom you have no connection has had the exact same personal experience as you have had. What I knew was: there are two of us within one persona. Of course, we can speak in terms of multiple "I's" and different selves within and circumstantially. But that is not what I am driving at. Each of us has within what might be called a plus and minus self. A self that is capable and focused; and a self that is shrinking and diffuse. The plus self is that which you experience when you realize that a task or effort you regarded with trepidation was entirely within your reach. It is the self that proves formidable even when you are induced to backslide into habitual doubt or morbid self-obsession. This greater self, when thrown on its own resources, finds solutions that during periods of fear seem doubtful and illusory—but prove entirely real and attainable. This positive self, I came to realize, is not a figure of speech or a compensatory fantasy. It is an actuality.

I came to see this further in an alluring 1900 instructional tale called *The Magic Story* by Frederick van Rensselaer Dey (1861–1922). Dey, a prolific detective-genre fiction writer, captured one of the most extraordinary truths of human nature, and created one of the strangest inspirational works ever written. Written in two parts, *The Magic Story* featured this theme of a positive double, which Dey called your "plus-entity." The tale depicts the life of a down-and-out seventeenth-century craftsman who discovers that a haunting presence, or other self, is hovering around his periphery. Dey's hero discovers that his counter-self is a real part of him, one that is "calm, steadfast, and self-reliant." As soon as he comes to identify, literally, with his plus-entity, his life is radically transformed for the better. "Make a daily and nightly companion of your plus-entity," the hero counsels.

Who is your plus-entity? Only you know for sure. It is the self you feel within as an alternative to your rote behaviors and reactions. You catch glimpses of this self, so you know that it is real. It is the self who calmly lays down the law with a violative person. It is the self who delivers on what was promised, regardless of unexpected disruptions. It is the self who assesses situations and acts with dispatch. It is the self who feels no need to preen but who nonetheless presents publicly with self-respect and earned knowingness. It is the self who moves progressively and persistently toward a cherished aim.

And this, finally, is why you cannot blurt out your aim or insights to random people and sometimes even to those to whom you are close: only you know the nature of your other self. Your opposing plus-entity is intimate. You alone know what needs it must fill and what calls it must answer. No sooner do you offer up to someone what you want, or who you want to be (the two are ultimately the same), than that person starts to pick it apart, and tell you, "No, it's in this direction not that one." That person may offer you contrary examples from his or her own experience, or, worse still, quote spiritual bromides: long-familiar, anodyne pointers that tell us how we are supposed to live.

My contention, as noted in the introduction, is that *we are supposed to live in the direction of self-expressiveness.* Without that you feel sorrow. With it you feel gravitationally pulled in the direction of victory, whether potential or realized. We rarely use terms today like victory, seeing such concepts as one-sided, narrow, oppressive, or illusory. Within the individual, however, victory is what is sought, and your heart will not rest easy until it is approached. Does victory ultimately satisfy? Much wisdom literature calls that into question. And it is a valid question. But, like the nature of money, it can never be addressed maturely without first experiencing it.

I must clarify that I am not counseling a go-it-alone attitude. When I caution against sharing your aim, I do not mean it in an exclusionary way but in a discretionary one. Recent to writing these words, I shared my aim with one of the people I trust most in life. She had some pointed and useful criticisms. I took them to heart. The exchange was valuable not only because of the quality and insight of her intellect, but also because I had been very selective only to share my aim with someone who I knew could provide a supportive and informed critique.

Finding your other self can be a fitful process. But it must begin with an absolute openness. And a personal belief or faith—which *in action* are termed persistence—that such a possibility exists.

This came home to me one evening when I was out with friends. As conversation buzzed around me, I was ruminating on some life issues, and from within I realized a principle, which reached me almost like a voice: "You are stronger than you think." I was struck by the indelible and provable fact of that statement not just for me but for everyone. It may sound ordinary but truth is simple and it arrives like a force. And what is true is never exactly ordinary but basic. This statement was, in effect, the voice of my other self. Was I transformed? Yes, quietly. The following day rather than waking up and chasing down all the little brushfires that I was sure were burning somewhere, I stepped back. What did I really want? And would frenetic activity get me there? Ralph Waldo Emerson made an intriguing observation in his essay "The Over-Soul" in 1841:

The things that are really for thee gravitate to thee. You are running to seek your friend. Let your feet run, but your mind need not. If you do not find him, will you not acquiesce that it is best you should not find him? for there is a power, which, as it is in you, is in him also, and could therefore very well bring you together, if it were for the best. You are preparing with eagerness to go and render a service to which your talent and your taste invite you, the love of men and the hope of fame. Has it not occurred to you that you have no right to go, unless you are equally willing to be prevented from going? O, believe, as thou livest, that every sound that is spoken over the round world, which thou oughtest to hear, will vibrate on thine ear! Every proverb, every book, every byword that belongs to thee for aid or comfort, shall surely come home through open or winding passages. Every friend whom not thy fantastic will, but the greater and tender heart in thee craveth, shall lock thee in his embrace.

Sometimes there is, and must be, strength in repose. This relates to one of the sixty-four six-lined symbols or hexagrams that make up the ancient Chinese oracle the *I-Ching*. The *I-Ching* uses the symbols of nature to convey meaning. For that reason, the ancient work makes a good source of parallel study to the practice of Cosmic Habit Force, which also seeks to detect and prescribe the patterns of nature. Hexagram six in the *I-Ching* is sometimes called "Calculated Inaction." Sinologist and translator John Blofeld described the meaning of this pictogram in his classic (though sometimes overlooked) 1968 analysis of the *I-Ching*:

> The significance of this hexagram is that inaction while awaiting the outcome of events will enable us to avoid a danger now threatening. Firmness, clarity of mind and success in winning the confidence of others are now demanded of us; with them, our undertakings will prosper. Moreover, this period of inaction is a good time in which to go on a journey or else for relaxation and enjoyment.

It is not always easy to find the right balance between repose and effort. At certain instances, the need for repose simply makes itself felt and outcome takes a secondary seat. I invite you to search for your plus self by sometimes stepping away from the ordinary approaches. It may be that some of us require greater repose—and some greater effort. Stark honesty alone will tell you. Without honesty, your positive entity will never be welcomed.

You may experience your positive entity as a knowingness or possibly as a physical sensation. The latter may, at first, seem alarming. But at such moments just be welcoming. It is only yourself that you are encountering, either metaphorically or perhaps in some more literal way. I learned in recent years that my only real fear on the path is of stagnancy or delusion. I do not want to mislead or misdirect myself or another. That alone is my cardinal rule. When something feels a bit scary, it is usually a sign of potency. Embrace it.

HABIT 20

Avoid Predatory Personalities

Earlier I quoted Napoleon Hill cautioning: "Avoid persons and circumstances which make you feel inferior." This simple remark contains greater dimensions than may at first appear.

One of the toughest lessons I have had to learn in life, and that I am still learning as I write these words, is the prevalence of people who are *emotionally predatory*. Such people use emotional powerplays—almost always with plausible deniability—to keep you unsteady, needful, or confused.

Emotional powerplays are vampiric. Such moves are the adjunct reality for which the mythical vampire is the metaphor. They must be watched for and, when discovered, separated from.

What I am writing took on a greater sense of urgency to me recently. I realized that the predatory personality—and I write this based on no data other than personal observation—probably composes something like fifty percent of the population. Shocking as that hypothesis sounds (although less so when perusing social media), it is why our culture abounds with terms like narcissist, bully, crazy maker, abuser, borderline personality, and so on. These terms and others denote the emotional predator, whose aim, sometimes unconsciously—which is of no pragmatic importance in terms of conduct—is to use force over another or derive a sense of power from another's suffering. Sometimes this thirst for force arises from a creative, physical, intimate, or financial deficit for which the aggressor compensates by destructive domination. The key thing is not to analyze this dynamic so much as to avoid it.

There exists a subset of this predatory personality, which might be identified under the rubric of *parasitical versus creative*. This variant appears in people who attach themselves to projects, institutions, or people to receive reflected glory. The thing sought may be reputation, image, opportunity, or money. There is nothing wrong with any of that provided another party *authentically contributes* to the quality of what is present and thus benefits symbiotically. The danger with the parasitical personality is that months or even years can pass before its nature as a taker versus a contributor becomes clear.

Predatory personalities are often cognitively and emotionally sophisticated. They may sustain periods of friendship and even intimacy for months or years: for as long as the arrangement delivers what they need. Despite the simulation of bonding, however, this person does not experience empathy. The predatory personality can read emotions—*but the only emotions that this persona experiences are his or her own*. Hence, such figures often prove insightful, shrewd, and possessed of well-constructed self-justification. They may even conceal their motives from themselves. In George MacDonald Fraser's ribald novel *Flashman* (1969), the antihero says: "I have observed, in the course of a dishonest life, that when a rogue is outlining a treacherous plan, he works harder to convince himself more than to move his hearers."

This dynamic also reveals why people sometimes form business partnerships only to discover years into their effort that their collaborator—someone who is perhaps a godparent to their kids, a personal confidant, or an advice-giver—has skimmed profits or committed fraud. This is sometimes revealed through a single event or gets detected across the arc of a pattern. When the reality comes to light, it creates so great a break with perception that the victim cannot immediately digest it. When digestion eventually occurs, and damage is assessed and mitigated, the betrayal itself may remain partly undigested, perhaps for a lifetime. This is understandable. The feeling that someone you trusted and shared intimacies with could also behave with duplicity may be impossible to fully accept. That is the aftereffect of predatory behavior.

Always remember: the emotional predator *recognizes emotions*—that is part of what makes him or her effective—*but experiences only his or her own emotions.* Hence, the person may possess a considerable emotional vocabulary and offer sound insights. But the predator *relates* only to what he or she goes through. This is why the person cannot see himself as a predator. The anger, sorrow, or need that they feel is their only emotive reality. This fuels a sense of rightness even as the predator acts in ways that may be ruthless. From the predatory perspective, all means are justified and rational.

Because this personality type is so prevalent, it may be, frankly, impossible to wholly avoid. You may find yourself dealing with short or long-term relationships with such figures at work, in families, in education, in the military, and so on. When you detect these relationships, do not blame yourself. But step around them carefully and separate as soon as you are able. This is easier done in institutional settings than in marriages or partnerships, of course, which may entail long-term crises to solve.

But you will do better at any sort of relational crisis, and I write this from both success and failure, if you do not blame yourself. I am not a diagnostician. I am a longtime and fitful student on the road of life, and nothing else. From that, I estimate that these personas, as noted, makeup perhaps half of the population. Hence, the issue is not: "why did this happen to me?"—rather, it is likely that it *will at some point happen*. Growth occurs when you discover it. And when you do, take steps not to allow such abuse to repeat. If you are like me, this may entail several false starts. Again, do not engage in self-blame; just act.

Emotionally predatory behavior can take so many different forms that it may appear innumerable in variety. But I will list the most prominent patterns, at least in my observation.

Subtle putdowns. Someone routinely drops rhetorical questions—"are you done with your Ph.D. yet?"—intended to subtly detract from your efforts or self-respect. The speaker often frames the statement in a manner that permits plausible denial of any intended offense. This *putdown-deniability* dynamic is, in fact, one of the giveaways of an emotional predator. If you detect this pattern, do not explain it away. Your aware-ness is a gift. Use it—and get away.

Insults. Someone references you, or your social group, in a demeaning or diminishing way. For example, the person may not use a derogatory term to your face but will say something historically disparaging about a neighborhood, school, affiliation, or group to which you belong or identify. Again, this behavior acts on plausible denial, the key tool of the predator. In other cases, the party may be cordial in person but will resort to slurs on social media.

Obfuscation. Someone repeatedly allows deadlines to slip, resists specificity about figures or dates, leaves appointments or plans unconfirmed, does not acknowl-edge timely communications, or adopts a posture of remove at critical moments. Purposeful obscuration keeps you unsteady. It is a powerplay. Reject it.

Ersatz communication. The other party, perhaps upon learning that you are unhappy about something, agrees to talk through the issues, but actually uses drawn-out or murky exchanges as a tactic of exhaus-tion, manipulation, or information seeking for his or her own purposes. All of the talk, sometimes across hours, produces no change, and presents a drain on your time. As a friend put it: "Some people use communication as a way to block communication." It is a control ploy.

Reversals. The predatory party seemingly gives in, agrees with you, and vows a change—but summarily breaks his or her word. The person may agree in principle or vow to fix something on "Monday morning"—and never acts on it.

Undelivered gifts or promises. The person offers you some possibility in terms of a job, assignment, or invitation—and then never raises it again. Exchanges go silent or drift into noncommittal verbiage. This keeps you in a suspended state of wanting. It keeps you at their disposal.

Ghosting. Communication freeze-outs are common to our era but, like all facets of human nature, they predate the digital age. Social technology exacerbates longstanding human crises. Let's say that someone initiates a relationship with you—and then drops you. Completely and without explanation. That is the ultimate predatory device. When you detect it, be glad that you have avoided a worse entanglement. That may not fully salve your heart but it is the truth. Nothing gives greater feelings of false power to the predator—filling a deficit that the person is unable to satisfy through relational or creative means—than attracting a friend, lover, collaborator, or confidant only to abruptly drop the person, thus creating bewilderment, doubt, and hurt. Cruelty empowers the predator.

*   *   *

When you discover an emotional predator, what step should you take? For one thing, do not confront the person. You will get nowhere. As noted, the predator always possesses, and will unfailingly use, plausible deniability. The confrontation will get turned against you ("you're too sensitive"; "you're overreacting"), and you will become a victim one more time. The chief thing is to acknowledge the truth to yourself and gently but firmly take steps to separate yourself. These steps may not occur immediately. There may be ties and bonds that cannot be easily severed. But your acknowledgment is critical. Inner conviction has a momentum of its own. Then, lay plans and quietly act on them.

I once prayed for wisdom. Wisdom is experience. I received experience. I write this chapter from no other place. If it matches your inner sensibility, use it.

HABIT 21

When You Meet a Cobra on the Road

I am going to share a personal story that is so blunt in detail it will leave you with no doubt that I am being transparent with you in this book. I make these disclosures purposefully not only to provide workable, vivid, and, I hope, relatable advice from the perspective of the search, but also because I abhor works of practical spirituality or self-help that evade difficult realities with familiar truisms, juiced-up stories, exaggerated data, concealed identities, or syrupy anecdotes. You deserve better. And you are going to get it.

Here is a story that most contemporary Americans have experienced in one fashion or another when dealing with private health insurance. Just before the Covid lockdown in early 2020, I transitioned to making Cobra payments on my health insurance plan. Due to bureaucratic snafus—or, more realistically, intentional policies—I found myself in a transitionary or "dead zone" of insurance for about two months. I paid premiums that were supposed to retroactively apply to those months; regardless, the carrier refused to reimburse about $900 in covered expenses. My "appeals" netted nothing but incredulity and stress. Many of you reading these words realize how insurance carriers use byzantine coding schemes and require multiple resubmission of claims to wear down consumers. In short, I was denied coverage for which I had paid. It is why I call health insurance "organized crime with a refrigerator magnet." I have no expectation that our political system will fix this any time soon. We are in it by ourselves.

While coping with the financial burdens of Covid, and wary of the experience just described, I made the difficult decision in March 2020 to discontinue my Cobra payments. But I received an unexpected—if temporary—reprieve. Under the federal government's Covid emergency guidelines, consumers received a one-year grace period on their Cobra payments. So, I was covered. After the grace term expired in April 2021, my Cobra administrator told me that if I resumed payments *from the date of their suspension* my insurance would remain intact. I followed the instructions and made the payments. But in June 2021, I was notified by snail mail that my insurance was canceled. A call-center rep could do no more than read off a script, telling me that—regardless of what I had been told weeks earlier—I now had to pay a lump sum of $10,000 in back premiums to remain covered. After consulting with my accountant and a friend who is a financial planner (and also part of my Master Mind group), I made the $10,000 cash payment. It severely cut into my liquid savings. It presented a financial crisis.

One evening in June 2021, I pondered what to do. I was at a loss. I felt on the edge of a precipice. I needed to earn more. But how?

Earlier in the day, on an unrelated issue, I had written this on Twitter: "Excellence is your only defense." A reader wrote me: "The question then is, how does one achieve excellence?"

I quoted him a passage from my book, *The Miracle of a Definite Chief Aim*:

In 1964, the spiritual teacher Jiddu Krishnamurti conducted a series of dialogues with young students in India. The teacher spoke of the dulling effect of conformity, and the need to live by your own inner light. A boy asked him: "How can we put into practice what you are telling us?" Krishnamurti replied that if we want something badly enough, we know exactly what to do. "When you meet a cobra on the road," the teacher said, "you don't ask 'What am I do to?' You understand very well the danger of a cobra and you stay away from it." Krishnamurti noted:

"You hear something which you think is right and you want to carry it out in your everyday life; so there is a gap between what you think and what you do, is there not? You think one thing, and you are doing something else. But you want to put into practice what you think, so there is this gap between action and thought; and then you ask how to bridge the gap, how to link your thinking to your action.

"Now, when you want to do something very much, you do it, don't you? When you want to go and play cricket, or do some other thing in which you are really interested, you find ways and means of doing it; you never ask how to put it into practice. You do it because you are eager, because your whole being, your mind and heart are in it."

As I reproduced this passage, I was struck by the immediate relevancy of Krishnamurti's words—as well as the congruency of the teacher's example of a cobra and my experience with . . . Cobra. I do not play word games but the proximity of message and metaphor struck me with poignancy.

Earlier the same day, I had been writing to a publisher about a book I wanted him to consider. In my draft email, I wrote: "money is not the most important factor . . ." After pondering Krishnamurti's passage, I felt compelled to revisit my note. I asked myself why I downplayed money. It occurred to me that it is the kind of line I have been writing, in one way or another, most of my adult life. If I am facing a cobra on the road—not literally but I am unprepared to say quite figuratively either—do I wish to get away from it *badly enough*? If so, then don't I, as Krishnamurti noted, *already know what to do*? Well, the first thing I did was cut that reference from my note. Money is important. It does not warrant disavowal or downplaying.

Earlier that same evening, I had been biking home over the Williamsburg Bridge, riding from the Lower East Side of Manhattan to my building in Brooklyn after taking one of my kids to a school orientation. As I crossed the bridge, I prayed for a financial solution. I have often prayed while crossing the body of water, the East River, which the bridge spans. Praying while crossing a river is a ritual for me. In doing so, I have frequently been delivered, although not always in expected ways. I prayed for a miracle that night, and I received one—of a sort. The realization about money that I just described—and the importance of not downplaying it—occurred immediately after I stashed my bike and entered my home. My miracle was not a pot of gold but a gauntlet of wisdom. Miracles are what we work for—and that work continues after they arrive. This miracle challenged me to use all my devices to escape the cobra on the road *if I really wanted to be free.*

The truth is, I have behaved somewhat gingerly toward money in my career. I have treated it with mild disdain and even fear, as if getting too close to it would seemingly sully my motives or give the misimpression that I am "money hungry" rather than dedicated to my ideas. Hence, I have often treated money as secondary, as I caught myself doing in my email. And, ironically, for all my efforts, including contributing back to organizations that host me, some people still harbor the point of view that I'm sticky fingered. This is due to a particular facet of human nature: *people see only those traits in others that they possess.* A shifty person does not understand or perceive honesty. He or she sees honesty as weakness or trickery. Whereas an honest person sees others as basically sincere and is shocked to get burned. *Everything is a mirror.*

In any case, after crossing the bridge, I realized that a new approach was necessary. But I had to *truly want* to adopt a new approach. And to want it so badly that it would *come naturally.* Was I prepared to exemplify my own counsel about an "attitude of earning" in Habit 14? Was I prepared to honor my own observations about "the force of necessity" in Habit 3? In pondering this, I knew that my challenge was not *mental* so much as *emotional*. Emotions are our ultimate rulers. This is especially true in matters of money and intimacy. But not in those alone. When facing a challenge, financial or otherwise, the question of whether you *absolutely want a solution* is the single greatest determinant of whether one will be found.

Wanting is foundational; but it is not the end of the equation. Wanting must be acted on with aplomb and skill, to which we now turn.

If you are a reader of Napoleon Hill, you are probably aware that in *Think and Grow Rich*, the author advises you to: 1) list a specific sum in connection with your aim; 2) name the date by which you intend to earn it; and 3) really *see and feel* that sum in your possession. In Habit 2, I counseled flexibility as to whether you name a sum. I do not regard it as orthodoxy. At the same time, flexibility does not mean avoidance. Hence, I want to revisit what Hill wrote—and how I acted on it in light of these events. In perhaps the most pivotal chapter of *Think and Grow Rich*, "Desire," Hill outlines six steps to attaining your goal:

First. Fix in your mind the *exact* amount of money you desire. It is not sufficient merely to say "I want plenty of money." Be definite as to the amount. (There is a psychological reason for definiteness which will be described in a subsequent chapter).

Second. Determine exactly what you intend to give in return for the money you desire. (There is no such reality as "something for nothing.")

Third. Establish a definite date when you intend to *possess* the money you desire.

Fourth. Create a definite plan for carrying out your desire, and begin *at once,* whether you are ready or not, to put this plan into *action*.

Fifth. Write out a clear, concise statement of the amount of money you intend to acquire, name the time limit for its acquisition, state what you intend to give in return for the money, and describe clearly the plan through which you intend to accumulate it.

Sixth. Read your written statement aloud, twice daily, once just before retiring at night, and once after arising in the morning. AS YOU READ— SEE AND FEEL AND BELIEVE YOURSELF ALREADY IN POSSESSION OF THE MONEY.

Hill adds a comment several lines later that I had neglected: "Only those who become 'money conscious' ever accumulate great riches. 'Money consciousness' means that the mind has become so thoroughly saturated with the desire of money, that one can see one's self already in possession of it." In one of my three editions of *Think and Grow Rich*, which I regularly read and markup, I included this undated margin note next to that passage: "This has been missing due to fear of loss—I agree too quickly." This relates to what I observed earlier about not wanting to appear overly attached to money. But Hill also writes: "You may as well know, right here, that you can never have riches in great quantities unless you can work yourself into a white heat of desire for money, and actually believe you will possess it."

This "white heat of desire" had also been missing—something the events I described laid bare. And began to reverse.

As it happens, several months before these events, I devised a monthly budget of what I required to lead a prosperous and secure financial life, one that provided for the needs of people I love and my own. I arrived at an ambitious but realistic yearly sum. In the past, I had worked with other sums that I wished to earn. In one case, the exact figure reached me within the time frame specified. But in other cases, I was working with sums that were too high to be realistic. To see yourself in possession of a sum, *you must believe that it is veritably within reach*. The figure can be substantial but not fantastical. Hill also writes that you should expect the figure to *accrue incrementally* between when you write it and your target date. Like most earnings, your figure gets parceled out.

When I returned to my budgeted figure, I discovered that I could now *see and feel it in my possession*. I had blocked it out carefully. I felt that I *deserved it* for the work I delivered. It is ambitious but reasonable. It is a sum that I can wrap my mind and emotions around.

In my earlier notes I wrote: "I begin progressively moving toward this Oct. 2020 and net this monthly avg. starting June 2021." As it happens, my target date coincided exactly with when I started writing this section. As of this writing, I did not reach my target; hence, I was compelled to reset my date. But I did not feel discouraged. This kind of reset should not be feared, avoided, or fretted over—it is a natural and, I would argue, progressive aspect of working with Hill's program. The key thing is: for the first time since I started rigorously working with *Think and Grow Rich* about eight years earlier, I could truly see and feel a budgeted, incremental, and renewable sum directly in my possession. As I write these words, I have accrued commitments that place me closer to my goal than any time since devising it.

My confidence stems from effort. You cannot viably pull a number from out of the ether of desire. You must sit down and map out a serious if ambitious budget of what level of income would cover your expenses keyed to a comfortable and happy existence. Your budget must account for the fundamentals with allocations for beauty, leisure, travel, and other forms of fulfillment, based upon your private definitions. In devising my budget, I used the following categories, which may require adjustment based on your lifestyle, geography, and values. I did not, for example, include auto expenses. I listed:

1. Rent
2. Health Insurance
3. Child Support
4. Child Extras
5. Dining
6. Savings
7. Charity/Contributions
8. Travel
9. Clothes
10. Sundry (repairs, etc.)
11. Research/Work-Based Services

I also added an additional $500 per month to cover unexpected needs, which always arise. From that sum, I determined the gross and net monthly, and thus yearly, income I required. The gross figure became my goal.

Hill also requires that you specify *what services you intend to deliver* to earn this figure. To that end, I listed an ambitious *but realistic* description of my work as a writer, speaker, and presenter. I also detailed the services or products I provide, such as books, talks, narration, articles, screen appearances, and consulting. I further named the human resources that allow me to provide these things, including collaborators, graphic artists, and capable representation. In sum, I determined: 1) what I wish to earn, 2) what I supply in exchange for it, and 3) the tools required to do so. Hence, I did not arrive at some errant sum but an authentic if bold figure.

The steps I just described enabled me to truly visualize this sum in my possession.

As you may have detected, I am providing the emotional and mental requisites needed to enact Hill's program. Absolute emotional dedication is the baseline. That dedication may prove more elusive than it first appears. Following dedication and determination, you must decide on an *informed* financial aim and be earnest about it. Will your financial aim come true? I have been starkly honest with you and I will continue to be. I have literally found no greater blueprint to success than Hill's program. Although I have criticisms of the man, you can find them in my *One Simple Idea* and in my introduction to *The Wisdom of Napoleon Hill*, it is why I remain dedicated to his work. My dedication rests on experience. And while you may need to adjust Hill's approach, as I have, I pledge to you that, yes, your aim will grow from his program, financial and otherwise. I have experienced too much validation to doubt it. I have gone from writing obscure articles in 2003 to my first book appearing six years later to a current CV that you can judge for yourself.

Try. Your efforts will not be in vain.

HABIT 22

Expect Great Things

I owe the title of this chapter to historian Kevin Dann. I was privileged to publish his biography of Henry David Thoreau which uses this title phrase, drawn from one of Thoreau's personal letters. To understand Thoreau's inner life and intellectual background, I know of no better guide than Kevin's study. The point of this penultimate chapter is to explore the habit of thought that Thoreau finds within this principle.

To that end, it is worthwhile reading Thoreau's letter in full, which is ostensibly related to botany—yet it says so much more:

Concord [MA] May 19th 1859

Miss Mary H. Brown,

Excuse me for not acknowledging before the receipt of your beautiful gift of may-flowers. The delay may prove that I did not fear I should forget it, though very busily engaged in surveying. The flowers were somewhat detained on the road, but they were not the less fragrant, and were very superior to any that we can show.

It chanced that on the very day they arrived, while surveying in the next town, I found more of these flowers than I have ever seen hereabouts, and I have accordingly named a certain path "May-flower Path" on my plan. But a botanist's experience is full of coincidences. If you think much about some flower which you never saw, you will be pretty sure to find it some day actually growing near by you. In the long run, we find what we expect. We shall be fortunate then if we expect great things.

Please remember me to your Father & Mother

Yours truly

Henry D. Thoreau

Expect great things. It is not always easy to direct the mind and emotions in the compass point of expectation. Hopeful expectancy, the trigger behind most placebo responses, is a mood state that comes and goes. This is why placebo researchers generally use a device, such as an inert substance or treatment, to trigger it. (Although new boundaries are being broken with "transparent placebo" experiments, which evoke a statistically significant healing response without using a decoy drug.) Like the weather, expectancy cannot always be cultivated. But the very act of effort can, in my experience, replicate the beneficial qualities of expectancy. And perhaps something more. The key factor is meaningful resilience. I want to illustrate this quality by quoting a passage about a personal experience from *One Simple Idea*, my 2014 study of the positive-mind movement:

In the first decade of this century, I spent several years within a spiritual group dedicated to the ideas of Russian philosopher G. I. Gurdjieff. I was under the guidance of a remarkable and very gifted teacher—a gruff, lovable man of razor-sharp intellect. He demanded the most from everyone around him, though no one so much as himself. He used to delight in giving my colleagues and me "impossible" tasks to perform. At every turn we found our mettle tested and our limits stretched.

One time in preparation for a winter camping trip, he instructed me to purchase some plastic buckets, for a choice purpose: to serve as chamber pots for those female campers who didn't want to venture outside of their tents into the icy woods at night. The buckets, he directed me, with glee, must be heart-shaped and colored pink. Or, as a second-best option, he allowed, they could be red. I began searching—visiting hardware and bed-bath stores in New York City.

No pink buckets could be found, and certainly no heart-shaped ones. I made calls and checked still more stores. Aside from receiving some odd looks, I turned up nothing. I fell back on looking for red plastic buckets, of an ordinary shape—not too difficult a task, it seemed. But, once more, in the commercial capital of the nation, no one seemed to have red plastic buckets for sale. By this point my wife was losing patience with me. Why, she wondered, didn't I show the same zeal for ordinary household projects as I did for this task? After more days of searching, it was final: I could find no pink, no red, and certainly no heart-shaped buckets. I would have to call up my teacher and say, "I tried, but I failed."

This phone call was on my mind just before I embarked on an errand at a small neighborhood grocery store near my home on Manhattan's East Side. I stood outside the store with my cellphone in my hand, but something told me: just wait, don't make the call right now. I went inside the store and walked straight to the back, to the cold-foods section. And there, at the rear of this modest, around-the-corner store, stood a pile of fresh, shiny plastic buckets—not only pink but also heart-shaped. I couldn't believe it. I stopped a stock boy and asked, "What color are those buckets?" Fixing me with the nut-of-the-day look, he replied: *Pink*. They had just arrived in, he said.

I cannot assert that my tireless search somehow manifested the yearned-for buckets. But nor can I call the situation ordinary. It's the kind of incident that a person has to be *involved* in, with some skin in the game: a situation in which you endeavor past all conventional effort, to the point where giving up seems like the only reasonable option, and the experience of then suddenly accomplishing an aim, or in this case finding an unlikely item in the unlikeliest of places, carries an emotional charge that no actuarial table can fully capture.

Statistics are wonderful for measuring odds, but not for measuring the emotional gravity that one attaches to them. It can be argued that emotions are incidental to odds. But not entirely. An event is notable not solely for its odds (and these odds were slim) but for the *quality of the event's meaning* given the expectations and needs of the individual. And at such times, an act of positive persistence seems to net a result that goes beyond ordinary cause and effect:

something *additional* seems to occur. Exceptional commitment appears to summon an exceptional factor, neither fully expected nor describable.

It is also possible to observe a contrary case—in which panic, impatience, or anxiety conspires to overturn all reasonable, positive odds, and foments a negative outcome. I purposely used a simple example above not to highlight life's most dramatic stakes but to illustrate something about the nature of an outlook within the confines of everyday existence. But we can also consider graver circumstances, on which a person's life depends.

Consider it a personal ethical experiment to allow for the prospect that Thoreau is right: *expectancy is determinative.* Seen in the light of how we are exploring the principle here, there is virtually no downside to erring on the side of possibility. Such an outlook requires no sacrifice of critical thought and invites no lapse of effort but rather the opposite. *Expectancy, for our purposes, is interchangeable with intelligent persistence, which cultivates it.* And expectancy may, in fact, be the critical emotional factor in delivering you to a needed thing or situation.

Psychologist Carl Jung noted the role that enthusiasm and expectancy can play in a thought system. Jung studied a series of ESP experiments conducted by Duke University researcher J.B. Rhine (1895–1980) in the

1930s. Rhine's subjects consistently, and inexplicably, scored higher "hits" on a deck of cards early in sessions when excitement and anticipation ran high. As time passed, accurate hits would taper off, though they could spike again if the subject's interest was newly aroused. Thus, reasoned Jung in his 1952 essay *Synchronicity*:

> Lack of interest and boredom are negative factors; enthusiasm, positive expectation, hope, and belief in the possibility of ESP make for good results and seem to be the real conditions which determine whether there are going to be any results at all.

Jung's observations amount to more than may initially be apparent. It is not always easy for twenty-first century readers to appreciate the stature in which experimental psychologist Rhine and his ESP tests were once held. For about a generation, from the early 1930s through the 1960s, Rhine was one of the most talked about scientists in America, a subject of public fascination and scholarly respect. Years of mostly polemical and tautological criticism have quieted the renown once associated with his name. For intrepid readers, however, Rhine's 1934 monograph, *Extra-Sensory Perception*, will still prove an extraordinary journey into the statistical findings he amassed in his ESP experiments with so-called Zener cards. Zener cards are a deck of 25 cards with five symbolic images (such as a circle, a cross, squiggly lines), which Rhine employed in tens of thousands of trials to track the persistence of higher-than-average hits among various subjects. Rhine's statistics and the conditions of his testing have been subjected to probably more scrutiny than any other lab-based psychological study; they have never been overturned. They have been replicated, as discussed in his book *Extra-Sensory Perception After Sixty Years*. But for the persistent controversy surrounding ESP in general, the Rhine experiments demonstrated, beyond evidentiary doubt, the occurrence of some kind of anomalous transfer of information in a laboratory setting. If ESP, or extra-physical data conveyance of some kind, does not exist, then the clinical model on which we base our data testing is itself flawed in some not yet understood way.

Rhine was so dedicated to eschewing any kind of sensationalism that he hesitated to draw conclusions from his own studies. In the British appendix to his classic 1934 work, Rhine, in the kind of quietly monumental communication that marked his style, did briefly remark on the effects of enthusiasm among subjects in his ESP lab:

Since my greatest interest is in stimulating others to repeat some of these experiments, I should like to mention here what has seemed to me to be the most important condition for ESP. This is a spontaneity of interest in doing it. The fresh interest in the act itself, like that of a child in playing a new game, seems to me the most favorable circumstance. Add now . . . the freedom from distraction, the absence of disturbing skepticism, the feeling of confidence or, at least, of some hope, and I think many good subjects can be found in any community or circle.

In effect, not only was the researcher commenting on advantageous circumstances for the occurrence of ESP, but his remarks amounted to a capsule playbook in the circumstances that cultivate any human achievement. Thoreau's instincts, Jung's analysis, and Rhine's data line up perfectly.

Expect great things. And you maintain this emotional state *by endeavoring great things*.

HABIT 23

The Habit of No Habits

This is our final habit. Its intent is to give you agency to violate *all habits*, including those in this book, unless they pass the trial of your own verification. Let me give you an idea of what drove me to this step—and why I am dedicated to it.

If you are like me, you probably look over old books you've read of spirituality, psychology, and philosophy, and check out the margin notes you made.

Sometimes these notes reflect old or outmoded attitudes; sometimes they are markers of the past that allow you to measure progress; or sometimes they are statements of problems or barriers that persist.

But I recently encountered a different kind of note: one that denotes "truths" in which I simply no longer believe.

Spiritual language is extremely powerful. It gets repeated conceptually across many generations. The popular language of spirituality—"ego," "attachment"—even the word "spirituality" itself—can appear to indicate given and unquestioned truths.

But concepts of the psyche must be open to question, always and in all ways.

Recent to this writing, I happened upon this margin note in a book, which I wrote about ten years earlier: "I fear that my ego-hunger for 'success' will overwhelm my search for the higher." I no longer believe in the assumptions behind any of those statements.

For one thing, notice how "off the shelf" that language is. All of its terminology denotes the assumption that there exists a greater, unseen life versus a temporal, ego-driven life. I recognize how persuasive that framework is. It undergirds much of Western and Eastern religious life. But is it true? Does it meet the needs of your insights, experience, and deepest wishes?

As noted, I have come to question the higher-lower paradigm. Today, I think in terms of self-expression, without vertical divisions. And where would such divisions even begin and end? Where does "ego" turn into something else? When does "essence" flip into "personality?" In any case, these are all metaphors—not descriptors of actuality.

Actual experience is hard-won. It is difficult to honor because it may (or may not) run counter to long-standing consensus or decisions found within spiritual traditions or literature about what is and is not true. Or experience may sync with those decisions. The point is: *it must be your own.*

Let me share what I hope will be an affirming episode in independent practice. On a winter afternoon in 2008, I climbed to the top of a stone tower on the banks of the Charles River in Weston, Massachusetts. The Victorian-era oddity was built in 1899 to commemorate a Viking settlement that some believe Norse explorer Leif Erikson founded on the banks of the Charles around 1,000 A.D.

Named Norumbega Tower, after the legendary settlement, the 38-foot column had iron bars on its windows and doors to keep out snoopers, ghost hunters, and beer-drinking high schoolers. All I knew was that I wanted to go inside. I slithered my six-foot-two-inch frame through a loose grill, discovered some graffiti left by devil-worshipping metalheads (Satan love them), and climbed a dank stone stairway to the top.

At that time in my life, I had one great desire burning in my heart: to become a writer. I had already been

active in this direction, but I was not young—I was
past 40. I swore from the top of that tower that I would
establish myself as a known writer. I asked all the forces
available to me on that frigid winter day, seen and
unseen, physical and extra-physical, to come to my aid.

Something swelled up within me at that moment:
I felt in sync physically, intellectually, and emotionally
and at one with my surroundings; my wish felt clear,
strong, and assured, as though lifted by some unseen
current. It was a totalizing experience, which went
beyond the ordinary. In the years immediately ahead,
I did become known as a writer—I was published by
Random House and other presses, won a PEN literary
award, and received bylines in places including *The New
York Times*, *The Wall Street Journal*, *Politico*, and *The
Washington Post*—publications not typically drawn to
the kinds of occult topics I pursue.

My act that winter day was entirely spontaneous and
spur of the moment. I did not plan or prepare for it, and
I was not reciting any ceremonies, spells, or rituals from
a book. It was an example of what I now call *anarchic
magick*. (I follow the alternate spelling of magick to dis-
tinguish it from stage magic.)

Having been through an orthodox bar mitzvah as a
kid, and much later spending eight years within a deeply
intellectual esoteric order, which demanded study,
memorization, and a grasp of profoundly arcane topics,

I have developed a yearning for freedom in my spiritual pursuits. I now have an allergy to the memorization of liturgy, passages, spells, ceremonies, arcana, and call-and-response recitations. I believe that focusing the will, directing the mental energies, synchronizing your mind, body, and emotions with the natural world, and, possibly, summoning unseen forces or entities— all things that are part of traditional ritualistic and ceremonial practice—are best approached, for me and others, in a mood of impulse, individual prerogative, and anything-goes effort.

This does not mean that I dismiss the study of esoteric and ethical philosophies—not at all. But once you have assimilated the rulebook, or many rulebooks as the case may be, you must throw them away and dance on the edges of your intuition. This was true in a different line of work for the twentieth century's great abstract visual artists, such as Pollock and Dali, who knew quite well how to paint portraiture but at the first possible moment vaulted past expectations. Metaphysical seekers should demonstrate the same agency.

In my view, anarchic magick, or the habit of no habits, means that you can, and sometimes must, abruptly depart one line of practice and just as abruptly begin another. Such a schismatic act can bring special power. Beginners and latecomers to any field often become its innovators. For a secular example, consider Gaston

Glock, the inventor and manufacturer of the Glock handgun. As explored in journalist Paul M. Barrett's *Glock: The Rise of America's Gun*, the Austrian engineer had, until well into middle age in the 1980s, dedicated his career to manufacturing curtain rods and knives. Glock knew almost nothing about firearms. But when the Austrian military issued a call for a sleek, new-generation sidearm, the inventor was intrigued. Not knowing what "couldn't" be done, Glock took three months to develop a working prototype of his lightweight plastic pistol, which went on to revolutionize handguns.

Embracing a pursuit belatedly—and proceeding to learn everything about it—spurs innovation and spurns prejudice, allowing you to leap past pitfalls and conventions and do things in a fresh way. This is as true in spirituality as in material matters.

I had the following exchange in an interview with the occult website and zine *Secret Transmissions*. It provides a good example of the types of practice anarchic magick encourages:

Q: Mythology is intimately intertwined with magic, whether it's Norse, Greek, Egyptian, Celtic or other. But let's say that you don't feel compelled to join a group ruled by a specific pantheon but are nevertheless deeply moved and inspired by these deities and want to make them a part of your spiritual life; how might that be achieved?

Well, to share a personal story, many years ago on Canal Street near Manhattan's Chinatown, I discovered an old office building that had a beautiful profile relief of Mercury above its entrance. Apropos of what I was saying earlier, I harbor questions about the lingering energies of the old gods.

I made a practice, for many weeks, of taking the subway to that slightly out-of-the-way place every morning and praying to that image of Mercury. I used to stand on the sidewalk in plain sight and pray in front of a very nice and indulgent Latin American woman who sold newspapers from on top of a milk crate in front of that building.

I don't know whether she thought I was crazy—there is a greater tolerance and embrace of occult religious methods in Latin America, so I might not have seemed very odd to her. In any case, I venerate the personage and principle of Mercury, and this was a means of expressing that, as well as petitioning favor. I felt some satisfaction, though no sense of conclusion, from this act.

I strongly believe that no one has to join anything, or seek validation from anyone when conducting an experiment. Traditions arise from experiment. I heartily encourage individual experimentation backed up by some kind of education and immersion in the history and practices of what you're attempting.

Never permit anyone to tell you that some kind of prerequisite is necessary to begin a spiritual practice—who is saying that, and what is the condition of his life that gives him authority to do so? Brush past experts and commence your search or practice *now*, wherever you like—do it with maturity, dedication, intellect, grit, and seriousness, but never be deterred by any kind of entry barrier.

Study your physical surroundings to detect your natural temple, or places where prayer, affirmations, setting of intentions, or appeals to a higher force may take place. I have already named two. I found another in the main branch of New York Public Library, where I occupied a research room recent to this writing. On the third floor of the beaux-arts building appears a ceiling mural of Prometheus, who stole fire from the gods and enlightened humanity. Prometheus is a cosmic figure with special relevance to strivers, seekers, and even Satanists.* Positioned around him on the floor below are marble lampposts with cloven hooves carved into

---

* I have an esoteric definition of the Satanic, which sees it as the force of rebellion, creative friction, and usurpation of limits, barriers, and calcified structures.

their base. In this setting, you can touch one of the cloven hooves, perhaps arousing your natural tendencies, and send Prometheus an intention or appeal for something you intensely desire. Are you willing to try this, or something like it, in your own surroundings? Or are you too "serious" to venture such a childlike exercise? The wish for respectability, observed spiritual teacher Jiddu Krishnamurti, is the greatest deterrent to selfhood and progress.

Some may wonder how what I am describing differs from chaos magick, the practice of asserting your will in self-devised and inventive ways. Well, I see my outlook as a cousin to chaos magick, but with an even greater emphasis on the do-it-yourself ethic. Everything that I cite here is an example: Throw it out and devise your own rituals. Share them only to inspire, not to instruct. Chaos magicians sometimes see their work from a psychological perspective; my path is spiritual.

Maybe it is a little inflated, but I am touched by the declaration of anarchist revolutionary Mikhail Bakunin (1814–1876): "I cleave to no system, I am a true seeker." I take that as the informal motto of anarchic magick.

I invite you to run past everything you know, forget all your "respectable" spiritualities—and see what you find. When you do find something—and I am confident that you will—do not coddle and nurse it for too long. Do not remain still. As Ralph Waldo Emerson, referencing the legend of Romulus and Remus, wrote at the opening of his 1841 essay "Self-Reliance":

> *Cast the bantling on the rocks*
> *Suckle him with the she-wolf's teat;*
> *Wintered with the hawk and fox,*
> *Power and speed be hands and feet.*

Allow today to be a day without assumptions or presumed limits; a day ruled only by your search. That is your innate right as an independent being.

Cosmic Habit Force, finally, favors individual agency, creativity, spontaneity, and meaningful impulse. These traits summon the powers of great expectation. The you that is both industrious and ebullient is the you who succeeds—and who nature favors. Now go and practice.

APPENDIX I

"The Law of Cosmic Habit Force"

(abridged from Napoleon Hill's *The Master Key to Riches*)

We now come to the analysis of the greatest of all of Nature's laws, the law of Cosmic Habit Force!

Briefly described, the law of Cosmic Habit Force is Nature's method of giving fixation to all habits so that they may carry on automatically once they have been set into motion—the habits of men the same as the habits of the universe.

Every man is where he is and what he is because of his established habits of thought and deed. The purpose of this entire philosophy is to aid the individual in the formation of the kind of habits that will transfer him from where he is to where he wishes to be.

Every scientist, and many laymen, know that Nature maintains a perfect balance between all the elements of matter and energy throughout the universe; that the entire universe is operated through an inexorable system of orderliness and habits that never vary, and cannot be altered by any form of human endeavor; that the five known realities of the universe are: (1) Time, (2) Space, (3) Energy, (4) Matter, and (5) Intelligence; these shaped the other known realities into orderliness and system based upon *fixed habits*.

These are nature's building-blocks with which she creates a grain of sand or the largest stars that float through space, and every other thing known to man, or that the mind of man can conceive.

These are the known realities, but not everyone has taken the time or the interest to ascertain that Cosmic Habit Force is the particular application of Energy with which Nature maintains the relationship between the atoms of matter, the stars and the planets in their ceaseless motion onward toward some unknown destiny, the seasons of the year, night and day, sickness and health, life and death. Cosmic Habit Force is the medium through which all habits and all human relationships are maintained in varying degrees of permanence, and the medium through which thought is translated into its physical equivalent in response to the desires and purposes of the individual.

But these truths are capable of proof, and one may count that hour sacred during which he discovers the inescapable truth that man is only an instrument through which higher powers than his own are projecting themselves. This entire philosophy is designed to lead one to this important discovery, and to enable him to make use of the knowledge it reveals, *by placing himself in harmony with the unseen forces of the universe, which may carry him inevitably into the success side of the great River of Life.*

The hour of this discovery should bring him within easy reach of the Master Key to all Riches!

Cosmic Habit Force is Nature's Comptroller through which all other natural laws are coordinated, organized, and operated through orderliness and system. Therefore it is the greatest of all natural laws.

The law of Cosmic Habit Force is Nature's own creation. It is the one universal principle through which order and system and harmony are carried out in the entire operation of the universe, from the largest star that hangs in the heavens to the smallest atoms of matter.

It is a power that is equally available to the weak and the strong, the rich and poor, the sick and well. It provides the solution to all human problems.

APPENDIX II

"Cosmic Habit Force"

(abridged from Napoleon Hill's *Think Your Way to Wealth*)

Cosmic Habit Force is the particular application of energy with which nature maintains the existing relationship between the atoms of matter, the stars and planets, the seasons of the year, night and day, sickness and health, life and death, and more important to us right now, it is the medium through which all habits and all human relationships are maintained, the medium through which thought is translated into its physical equivalent.

You, of course, know that nature maintains a perfect balance between all the elements of matter and energy throughout the universe. You can see the stars and planets move with perfect precision, each keeping its own place in time and space, year-in and year-out. You can see the seasons of the year come and go with perfect regularity. You can see that night and day follow each other in unending regularity.

You can see that an oak tree grows from an acorn, and a pine grows from the seed of its ancestor. An acorn never produces a pine, nor does a pinecone ever produce an oak, and nothing is ever produced that does not have its antecedents in something else which preceded it.

These are simple facts that anyone can see, but what most people cannot see or understand is the universal law through which nature maintains perfect balance between all matter and energy throughout the universe forcing every living thing to reproduce itself.

We caught a fragmentary glimpse of this great law of nature, which holds our little Earth in its proper position and causes all material objects to be attracted toward the center of the Earth when Newton discovered what he called the Law of Gravitation.

And if Newton had gone a few steps beyond where he stopped, perhaps he would have discovered that the same law which holds our little Earth in space and relates it to all the other planets in both time and space, relates human beings to one another in exact conformity with the nature of their own thoughts, he would have discovered that the same force which draws all material things toward the center of this Earth also builds man's thought habits in varying degrees of permanency.

He would have discovered that negative thought habits of whatever nature attract to their creator physical manifestations corresponding to their nature as perfectly as nature germinates the seed of the acorn and develops it into an oak tree.

Also, he would have discovered that positive thoughts reach out through the self-same law and attract physical counterparts of their nature. We are here concerned only with the method by which nature takes a hold on the mind through the operation of the law.

Before we go any further, let us briefly describe an important function of Cosmic Habit Force through which it controls all human relationships and determines whether an individual will be a success or a failure in his chosen occupation. This description can best be made by the statement that nature uses this law as a medium by which every living thing is forced to take on and become a part of the environment in which it lives and moves daily.

We are ruled by habits, all of us. Our habits are fastened upon us by repetition of thought and experience, therefore, we can control our earthly destinies just to the extent that we control our thoughts. It is a profoundly significant fact that over the power of thought a person may have complete control. Everything else is subject to forces outside of one's control. Nature has given man the privilege of controlling his thoughts, but she has also subjected him to the power of Cosmic Habit Force through which his thoughts are made to clothe themselves in their physical likeness and equivalent.

If a man's dominating thoughts are of poverty, the law translates those thoughts into physical terms of misery and want. If a man's dominating thoughts are of opulence, the law transforms them into their physical counterpart. Man builds the pattern through his thoughts, but Cosmic Habit Force works that pattern into its physical likeness and builds it into permanency.

"But how can a law of nature make something out of nothing?" some will ask. It is but natural that any practical person would want to know the exact manner in which, for example, Cosmic Habit Force could transmute thoughts of opulence into material riches or thoughts of poverty into material evidence of poverty. We are happy to raise the question and to answer it.

To begin with, let us recognize the fact that Cosmic Habit Force is silent, unseen, and unfelt and works in complete harmony with all of nature's other forces such as gravitation, electricity, evolution, etc., but it differs from all other natural forces in that it is the sole source of their power and serves as nature's controller through which every form of power and every law of nature must work. It is the master key to the universe, so great in power that it controls every living thing and every atom of matter, the control being carried out through established habit force.

The method by which Cosmic Habit Force converts a positive impulse or mental desire into its physical equivalent is simple. It merely intensifies the desire into a state of mind known as faith, which inspires one to create definite plans for the attainment of whatever is desired, the plans being carried out through whatever natural methods the resourcefulness of the individual can command. Cosmic Habit Force does not undertake to transmute the desires for money directly into bank balances but it does set into motion the mechanism of imagination through which the most easily available means of converting the desire into money is provided in the form of a definite idea, plan, or method of procedure.

This force works no miracles, makes no attempt to create something out of nothing, but it does help an individual, nay it forces him to proceed naturally and logically to convert his thoughts into their physical equivalent by using all the natural media available to him which may serve his purpose. The force works so quietly that the individual, unless he is of a philosophical trend of mind, does not recognize his relationship to what is happening to him.

On one occasion, an idea will present itself to his mind in a form that he calls a hunch, and it will inspire him with such definite faith that he will begin at once to act upon it. His entire being has been changed from a negative to a positive state of mind with the result that related ideas flow into his mind more freely. The plans he creates are more definite, and his words have more influence with other people.

Because he does not understand the source from which his hunch came, he may dismiss the matter and imagine the newly discovered idea or plan with which he achieves success was the creation of his own brain. The hunch is simply a desire that has been given the intensity to enable Cosmic Habit Force to take it over and give it the necessary momentum to convert it into a definite idea or plan of action.

From that point on, the individual must move on his own by using such opportunities, human relationships, and physical conveniences as may be available to him for carrying out his desire. At times, one is inspired with awe by the coincidental combination of favorable circumstances with which he is favored in carrying out his plans such as voluntary cooperation from unexpected sources, some fortunate transaction in business that provides unexpected money, etc., but always these strange and unexplained things happen through perfectly natural procedure similar to daily experiences.

What the individual cannot see or understand is the method by which Cosmic Habit Force gives to one's thoughts that peculiar quality, which gives them the power to surmount all difficulties, overcome all resistances, and achieve seemingly unattainable ends through simple but natural procedure.

That is one secret of nature that is not yet revealed, but neither has she revealed the secret by which she causes a seed of wheat to germinate, grow, and reproduce itself bringing back with it 100 additional grains for good measure.

Cosmic Habit Force guided me through an awe-inspiring maze of experiences before revealing itself to me. All through those years of struggle, there was one definite purpose uppermost in my mind, the burning desire to organize a philosophy with which the average man can become self-determining. Nature had no alternative but that of yielding to me the working principle of Cosmic Habit Force because I unwittingly complied with the law by persistently seeking the way to its discovery. If I'd known of the existence of the law and of its working principle at the beginning of my research, I could have organized the Philosophy of American Achievement in a much shorter period of time.

It is profoundly significant that the Law of Cosmic Habit Force was revealed after a daily contact of minds through the Master Mind Principle covering a period of almost two years. A major portion of this time was devoted to the analysis of problems which had nothing to do with the voluntary search for the law, but the important thing I wish here to emphasize is the fact that our habit of bringing our minds into rapport for a definite purpose daily actually had the effect of giving us the benefit of Cosmic Habit Force before we knew of the existence of the law.

If your life is not what you wish it to be, you can truthfully say that you drifted into your present, unhappy condition through the irresistible force of Cosmic Habit Force, but you cannot stop there because you shall know presently that time and Definiteness of Purpose backed by Cosmic Habit Force, can give you rebirth no matter who you are or what may be your circumstances.

You may be in prison without friends or money with a life sentence hanging over you, but you can walk through the front gate and back to the outside world of free men if you adapt yourself to this force in the proper manner. How do I know this can be done? Because it has been done before, because your common sense will tell you that it can be done once you understand the working principle and catch the full significance of its relationship to time and Definiteness of Purpose.

You may be suffering with ill health, which prevents you from using your mind. In that event, unless your illness is of a nature that can be cured, you may not be able to order your life just as you would have it, but you can make changes that will give you ample compensation for your trouble in living.

You're going to make another outstanding discovery in connection with this force. You're going to learn that every failure brings with it the seed of an equivalent advantage. You're going to discover beyond any room for doubt that every experience, every circumstance of your life is a potential steppingstone or stumbling block due entirely to the manner in which you react to the circumstance in your own mind.

You are going to discover that your only limitations are those that you set up in your own mind, but more important still, you're going to know that your mind can remove all limitations it establishes. You're going to know that you may be the master of your fate, the captain of your soul because you can control your own thoughts.

You are going to learn that failure is one of nature's methods by which he breaks up the grip of Cosmic Habit Force and releases the mind for a new start. You are going to understand that nature breaks the grip of Cosmic Habit Force on human beings through illness that forces them to rest the organs of the body and the brain. You are going to understand, too, that nature breaks the grip of the law on the people of an entire nation through wars and economic collapses known as depressions, thereby breaking up the monopolies and opportunity and reducing all men to substantially the same level.

I have given you a working knowledge of the relationship between Cosmic Habit Force, drifting, time, and Definiteness of Purpose. I have shown you through illustrations based on actual experience exactly how and why 98 out of every 100 people are failures.

I want you to know that the failures of life become such because they fall into the habit of drifting on all matters affecting their economic life, that Cosmic Habit Force carries them swiftly along in this drifting path until time fastens the habit permanently, after which there can be no escape except through some circumstance of catastrophe which breaks up their established habits and gives them an opportunity to move with Definiteness of Purpose.

I wish you to see that you are where you are and what you are today because of the influences which have reached your mind through your daily environment plus the state of mind in which you have reacted to these influences. I wish you to see and to understand that you can move with purpose and make your environment to order, or you can drift with circumstances and allow your environment to control you.

In both cases, Cosmic Habit Force is an irresistible force. It carries you swiftly toward a definite goal if you have one, and if you are definitely determined to reach that goal, or if you have no goal, it forces you to drift with time and circumstances until you become the victim of every stray wind of chance that crosses your path.

Everything in life worth having has a definite price upon it. There is no such reality as something for nothing. Having had the full advantage of studying Emerson's conclusions on this subject, plus the advantage of analyzing men and women representing the great successes and the outstanding failures, I am prepared to describe why every desirable thing in life has a price that must be paid, but I cannot pass this information onto the person who is not willing to face facts and admit to his own shortcomings. A willingness to look at oneself through unbiased eyes is a part of the price one must pay for the formula that leads to self-determination spiritually, economically, and physically.

Every person who succeeds must make use of some combination of the principles of this philosophy. The power that gives life and action to these principles is Cosmic Habit Force. Whenever any combination of the principles has been used successfully, as far as I have been able to determine by my research and personal experience, the law was unconsciously applied. I mean by this that those who have made successful application of the law have done so by mere chance without recognizing the real source of the power back of their achievements.

Observe the importance of the element of time as an essential factor with which the Principles of Achievement and Cosmic Habit Force becomes related. Cosmic Habit Force is so inexorable that it automatically takes over habits and makes them permanent.

If Cosmic Habit Force crystallizes an impulsive thought of illness and pain into a habit, think how much more quickly it will translate into permanency the pleasant, positive sensations of life. When nature has a message to convey to mankind, she does not release it to those who are indulging in dissipation, nor does she hand it over to those who have been pampered and protected from struggle, but she picks as her torch bearers those who have been seasoned by defeat until they have become self-determining.

This is your destiny. Embark on it.

APPENDIX III

Napoleon Hill's
17 Laws of Success

Over the course of his career, Napoleon Hill postulated 17 laws of success: these traits, Hill observed, appear in the life of almost any exceptional person. Although it is important to understand all 17 principles, the qualities of the whole are, in a sense, inherent within each one, the same way a primeval forest may be traced back to a single acorn. Since this book draws upon a teaching by Napoleon Hill, I thought it would be useful to have an outline of his overall steps.

1. **Definite Purpose**. The starting point of all achievement is one definite, passionate, and specific aim.

This is no ordinary desire, but something you are prepared to dedicate your life to. Your aim must be written down, read daily, acted upon constantly, and held in your heart with total commitment. If you are in earnest about it, this will come naturally.

2. **Master Mind**. This is a harmonious alliance ranging from as few as two to as many as seven people who meet at regular intervals to exchange ideas, advice, and sometimes meditations and prayers for one another's fulfillment. The Master Mind is critical to your success, as the pooling of intellects results in heightened insight, acumen, and intuition for all members.

3. **Applied Faith**. Faith is learnable. It is the ability to believe in and progress toward a goal based on the steady application of valid and productive principles. It is the understanding that what you achieve on a micro scale can be repeated on a macro scale. Seen in a certain way, faith is *intelligent persistence*. It is the gelling factor that aids all of your efforts.

4. **Going the Extra Mile**. You are most efficient, and will more quickly and easily succeed, when you dedicate yourself to work that you love and that you find indistinguishable from leisure or play. When

you work with this kind of passion, the quality and quantity of your output improves and you naturally do *more* and *better* work than you are paid for. This is why you owe it to yourself to find the work that you most like—and express that work by always going the extra mile for clients, customers, and employers.

5. **Positive Mental Attitude (PMA)**. As explored in Habit 1, This does not mean blocking out bad news or cultivating an unrealistically rosy mindset. Rather, it means believing in your reserves of resilience, using every positive tool at hand to approach your goals, and evaluating circumstances based on their potential for aiding your growth. People with PMA naturally attract others and become leaders.

6. **Initiative**. Leadership is essential to success—and *initiative* is the core of leadership. Initiative means *doing what ought to be done without being told to*. Only those who practice initiative become self-starters, examples to others, and high achievers. Initiative is one of Hill's simplest (if not easiest) laws; its practice is transformative.

7. **Enthusiasm**. Without enthusiasm nothing is possible. With it, you demonstrate acts of tireless commitment, which sometimes seem extraordi-

nary. This is why your Definite Chief Aim must tap
your passions. Enthusiasm is the closest thing life
grants us to a magic elixir.

8. **Pleasing Personality**. Your personality is the sum
total of your characteristics and appearance: the
clothes you wear, your facial expressions, the vitality of your body, your handshake, your tone of voice,
your diplomacy, your thoughts, and *the character you
have developed by those thoughts*.

9. **Accurate Thinking**. Accurate thought is vital to success. Thinking accurately means relying on facts,
observations, experience, and data that are relevant
to your aim. This means shunning gossip, rumor,
hearsay, idle talk, and—above all—casual opinions
from people who know little or nothing about your
field.

10. **Profiting by Failure**. What we call failure is often
temporary defeat. Temporary defeat frequently
proves a blessing because it jolts us and redirects
our energies along more desirable paths. Reversals,
setbacks, and temporary defeat impel the success-
driven person toward improved actions and plans.
Never miss an opportunity to review a disappointment for practical lessons and fresh approaches.

11. **Budgeting of Time and Money**. A friend once observed, "If you don't know how much money you have, you probably know very little else." You must keep track of and budget your two most precious outer resources: time and money. This means making a regular schedule of saving and paying down debts. It also means bringing orderliness to your tasks, knowing when to release a time-wasting activity and honoring deadlines. Time is the one resource that no one can replenish or replace.

12. **Self-Discipline**. Self-discipline or self-control is the force through which your enthusiasm is directed toward constructive ends. Without self-control—in speech, action, and thought—your enthusiasm is like unharnessed lightning: it may strike anywhere. The successful person combines both *enthusiasm* and *self-discipline*

13. **Controlled Attention**. This law relates to the two previous ones. You simply cannot afford the luxuries of a wandering mind (not always easy in the digital age) or procrastination. The latter is usually a form of fear, and it can be addressed through several of the methods explored in this book, including appeals to a Greater Force and possession of a Defi-

nite Chief Aim. "A man is what he thinks about all day long," wrote Emerson.

14. **Teamwork**. Success cannot be attained singlehandedly. It requires teamwork and cooperative effort. If your work is based upon cooperation rather than competition, you will go places faster and enjoy an additional reward in reduced stress and anxieties. To win the cooperation of others you must also offer them a strong motive or reward.

15. **Sound Health**. If you maintain indulgent habits of food, alcohol, or other intoxicants, these things will ultimately take over your time, your health, and your life. Your work and aims will eventually wither if you do not maintain reasonable habits of eating, rest, and exercise. If you do not pay adequate attention to your health now the consequences will take all of your attention later.

16. **Creative Vision**. Creative vision and imagination are the visualizing faculties that formulate your plans and *connect knowledge with new ideas*. Imagination and vision are not the equivalent of daydreams or escapism. Your imagination must be primed with credible information and facts, which it will then shape into ideas and applications.

17. **Cosmic Habit Force**. As explored in this book, this is one of Hill's most transformative principles. If you can train your habits of thought, emotion, and body along the lines of all the laws outlined above, an additional force—call it Infinite Intelligence, the Over-Soul, or Cosmic Habit Force—will lend itself to your efforts and expand everything you do. Cosmic Habit Force enlarges who you are. It is the energy through which life replicates itself through established channels. Function within the positive channels through which you wish to express your life and Cosmic Habit Force will aid your advancement.

INDEX

ABOUT THE AUTHOR

One of the today's most literate voices in self-help, **Mitch Horowitz** is a writer-in-residence at the New York Public Library, lecturer-in-residence at the Philosophical Research Society in Los Angeles, and the PEN Award-winning author of books including *Occult America; One Simple Idea; The Miracle Club*; and the G&D Media titles *The Miracle Habits* and *The Miracle Month*. Mitch has written on everything from the war on witches to the secret life of Ronald Reagan for *The New* York *Times, The Wall Street Journal, The Washington Post, Salon*, Time.com, and *Politico. The Washington Post* says Mitch "treats esoteric ideas and movements with an even-handed intellectual studiousness that is too often lost in today's raised-voice discussions." He narrates popular audio books including G&D Media's series of Condensed Classics. Mitch has discussed alternative spirituality on VICE News, CBS Sunday Morning, Dateline NBC, CNN, and throughout the national media. Mitch's book *Awakened Mind* is one of the first works of New Thought translated into Arabic. The Chinese government has censored his work. Visit him online at MitchHorowitz .com, on Twitter @MitchHorowitz, and on Instagram @MitchHorowitz23.

This book is also available in a G&D Audio edition narrated by the author.

9 781722 506339